# Coming Back From Heartbreak

*The story of one woman's trek
from loss to contentment*

Gaynor Morrissey

Copyright © Gaynor Morrissey 2022

All rights reserved. No part of this publication may be reproduced, distributed, or transmitted in any form or by any means, including photocopying, recording, or other electronic, or mechanical methods, without the prior written permission of the author or publisher, except in the case of brief quotations embodied in reviews and certain other non-commercial uses permitted by copyright law.

This publication is designed to provide accurate and authoritative information regarding the subject matter covered. It is sold with the understanding that the author or publisher is not engaged in rendering legal, accounting, or other professional services. If legal advice or other expert assistance is required, the services of a competent professional person should be sought.

ISBN Kindle: 978-0-473-66435-0
ISBN Paperback: 978-0-473-66433-6
ISBN Hardcover: 978-0-473-66434-3

Cover Design: Studio Monday www.studiomonday.co.nz

Printed in New Zealand and the United States of America

*... for Wendy, Sandra, Amber, Denise, Vicki and all the other warrior women in my life who, in their own unique ways, supported me through this trek.*

# Table of Contents

Chapter One: The Nuclear Explosion .................................................. 1
   *Trust Your Gut* ............................................................................. 4
Chapter Two: This Room Has A Huge Elephant In It ................... 6
Chapter Three: Stop The World ~ It's Time To Get Off ................ 10
   *Accepting Help* .......................................................................... 12
Chapter Four: Who Said I Have To Decide Now? ....................... 15
Chapter Five: Pause. Don't Rush Into Anything ........................... 18
   *The "T" Junctions In The Road Of Life* ................................. 22
Chapter Six: Take A Deep Breath .................................................... 23
   *Take Stock, Pause, And See If You Can Forgive* .................. 25
Chapter Seven: This Is Hell And I Can't Get Out ........................ 27
Chapter Eight: No Matter How Hard Things Seem, You Can And You Will Get Through It .................................................................. 32
Chapter Nine: Is Having History Enough? .................................... 35
Chapter Ten: Perfect Ingredients For Disaster ............................. 40
Chapter Eleven: Facing The Difficult Decisions ........................... 42
Chapter Twelve: No Change ............................................................ 43
   *One Day At A Time* .................................................................. 45
Chapter Thirteen: But What To Do Next? ..................................... 46
Chapter Fourteen: The Night Of The Real Separation ............... 48
Chapter Fifteen: Time To Take Stock ............................................. 51
Chapter Sixteen: Am I Brave Enough To Face The Reality? ...... 54

Chapter Seventeen: Confrontation Time .................................................. 57

Chapter Eighteen: Retreat ~ Regroup ..................................................... 61

Chapter Nineteen: Maybe There Is Hope ................................................ 65

Chapter Twenty: It Gets Real .................................................................. 67

Chapter Twenty-One: I Finally See The Pattern ..................................... 72

Chapter Twenty-Two: Finally Facing The Reality ................................... 74

*Self-Protection* .................................................................................. 78

Chapter Twenty-Three: Following My Moral Compass .......................... 81

Chapter Twenty-Four: First Steps Of The Rebuild ................................. 85

*First Steps* ........................................................................................ 88

Chapter Twenty-Five: Careful With The Spending! ............................... 90

Chapter Twenty-Six: What About Friends And Family? ........................ 94

*The Awkwardness – What To Say?* .................................................. 97

Chapter Twenty-Seven: His Life Pattern Was There For Me To See – But I Was Blind ................................................................................... 99

Chapter Twenty-Eight: What Happened? I Thought Things Were Good .................................................................................................... 102

*The Other Grass Is Always Greener* .............................................. 106

Chapter Twenty-Nine: Am I Responsible? ........................................... 108

Chapter Thirty: Unshackling The Chains .............................................. 115

Chapter Thirty-One: Starting To Let Go ............................................... 118

Chapter Thirty-Two: Picking Up That First Brick In The Rebuild ....... 120

Chapter Thirty-Three: I Might Make It! ............................................... 122

Chapter Thirty-Four: Is It Possible To Be Truly Happy Again? ........... 129

*This is Magic!* .................................................................................. 132

Chapter Thirty-Five: Do I Have To Forgive? ................................. 136

Chapter Thirty-Six: Some Help Along The Way .......................... 144

Chapter Thirty-Seven: Some Relationships Are Just Crap ............. 147

   *Different Endings* .................................................................. 148

Chapter Thirty-Eight: Reflections: What Can We Do Differently?. 149

Chapter Thirty-Nine: Being Right. Look Out, This One's A Real Kicker................................................................................................ 152

   *Change Is Possible* ................................................................ 158

   *Avoiding The Rabbit Hole* ..................................................... 160

   *Some Helpful Steps To Feeling Better* .................................. 163

Chapter Forty: Is It Time To Stick My Toe In The Water...Again?.. 168

Chapter Forty-One: In Our Lives For A Reason Or A Season ......... 174

   *Food For Thought* ................................................................. 177

Chapter Forty-Two: Karma And Forgiveness. Do They Go Hand-In-Hand?........................................................................................... 181

Chapter Forty-Three: Can A Couple Be Okay With Each Other After Divorce? ............................................................................................ 190

Chapter Forty-Four: Meet Hubby #1 .............................................. 193

Chapter Forty-Five: How Are Things Now? ................................... 197

Epilogue ........................................................................................... 200

# Chapter One

# The Nuclear Explosion

*"You're right... I have been with her... and I love her..."*

Eleven words I never thought I would hear from the man I had known for half my life. My husband.

I was struck by total disbelief. I felt as if I had just been shot. A verbal bullet straight to my heart halted everything I had known at that point in my life.

I could not believe what I had just heard, and I needed to somehow make sense of the words because they did not seem real.

Years of togetherness and life building and trust were shattered in those few seconds it took for him to utter those words.

Maybe he said them because I had cornered him; I was the one who had pushed for truth. I needed clarity. My heart had been plagued by suspicion and I needed the truth. I somehow thought laying it on the table would give me calm.

The instinct that something was wrong had not left me for some weeks and it had built inside me to the point of explosion.

There was that precise moment when I knew I had had enough.

There was no indecision. No hesitation.

I didn't intend to leave a detailed voice message—rather something along the lines of "Call me. I need to talk to you,"—but my thoughts had flooded out.

My husband, Grant, had gone to Auckland City, after a weekend at our home some six hours away. I was alone at our home and couldn't wait a second longer. This feeling that had been gnawing away, slowly building, had reached boiling point.

No stopping now.

Instinct told me that there was more to his 'friendship' with an old girlfriend who had been communicating with him than he was letting on.

A year or so earlier, when he told me that she had made contact, I had no problem with that. When he said that she'd be in town with her family and wanted to meet him for coffee and a catch-up, I had no problem with that either. He even invited me along. I was totally fine with him going alone. He had told me about her when we shared about previous relationships, and he hadn't ranked her that highly at the time. There were at least three other women he said had had a greater impact on his life, and each he had cared for deeply. This one had taught him to ski; they'd had a relationship and she was 'very nice'—but it wasn't enough for him to keep going with it. That was how he had described their time together.

After that meetup, and over time, he would mention that he had received an email from Rachel for Christmas, or she'd sent a birthday wish, and she had randomly chatted about her family, and asked after his.

So innocent.

When I found out that this communication was happening more frequently, I asked him if there was anything I needed to know, anything I needed to be concerned about, and his denials had pacified me.

But over time, he seemed to change. I sensed he was a bit 'different'. The changes were subtle. He became a little distant. He also became critical of me and started pointing out tiny faults or errors. He became less communicative about the more serious things in our life. He started to check his mobile screen first before answering a call. This was different; he usually just answered. Small changes. But those small changes added up, and stacked together they set off my radar.

**A LEARNING MOMENT**

***TRUST YOUR GUT***

Never discredit your gut instinct.

Your body can pick up on energy vibrations.

If something deep inside us alerts us about a person or situation, we should honor our instincts and never override them.

Just pause for a second before responding.

Always trust yourself and your ability to sense when something is not right.

You are not paranoid.

Your instinct flashes for a reason.

"You can feel when someone isn't being real with you..."

QUOTES4SHARING.COM

## Chapter Two

## This Room Has A Huge Elephant In It...

And so, I vomited out my thoughts and concerns in this voice-mail message I left for him on a mid-spring afternoon. I told him that my instincts were screaming at me that something was going on, and I named it. I thought it was about Rachel. I asked him to call me back.

Sometime later, he responded.

My heart started to pound.

His voice sounded sort of formal and his response seemed distant, as though he was talking to a stranger. And then he said those few words which, from that moment on, spun around and around in my head like a stuck song:

"...I have been with her... and I love her..."

Life's a funny thing. Some of the years of my life had merged into blurs with random highs and lows and a few stand—out memories. But then there are some moments that are incredibly vivid. The sounds, the smells... the motions around me... Kind of like when people say, "Where were you when John Lennon was shot?" or "What were you doing when 911 happened, or when Queen Elizabeth II passed away," and you know exactly where you were, how old you were, and what you were doing.

For me, this was one of those moments.

His words hung in the air. Powerful, yet surreal.

I couldn't believe that he conveyed this explosive news over the phone. And that he never actually confessed to me what was going on. Rather, he had responded to my point—blank accusation. I had to accuse him. He never fessed up or had the conviction to tell me. I had to be the one to lay the topic bare.

But the nuclear bomb had gone off. Shock waves reverberated from the walls. Time stood still.

The call must have ended, because the phone was dead. Our beautiful Weimaraner dog, Sabre, left his sleeping mat and gently laid his head on my arm, as he looked up at me with deep concern in his eyes.

I heard wailing. The sound was separate— it seemed distant— but I realized that it came from inside me. A sharp intake of breath ripped through my chest, and the noise of that made me aware that I hadn't been breathing.

I felt physically crushed by the brutality of the sharp pain in my chest. So unbelievably heavy. So darkly intense. I could not move. My body must have been on autopilot 'cos I was still alive but I felt like life had stopped. Everything had ceased for me. Closed down.

Dusk turned to dark and I was alone in our home—a rural property miles from anywhere or anyone.

Somehow, I found myself in bed, overcome by blackness and torment.

Every instinct within me was right about him and his girlfriend from so many years earlier.

*Rachel.*

I didn't want to be right.

At that moment I did not care how long this had been going on with her. All I knew was that the thirty-plus years he had been in my life (not all as my husband) must have ranked lower for him than the rush of new feelings… the fresh lust he must have been experiencing for this woman.

The intensity of the realization was so overpowering that I feared I might not physically survive this. Darkness crept over me, and the fear that I might not make it through the night became very real.

But somehow, I survived that night. Alone, surrounded by native bush, miles from any other homestead. Just silence. Darkness. And our loyal and beloved dog guarding me as my world, solidly built over so many years, was crumbling.

Those that have experienced life-altering, soul-shaking shock know what I am talking about here.

The new day shed light that revealed the stark truth. There was a blissful, surreal fuzziness—it could have been a dream—before I awoke to the knockout punch.

This is real.

## Chapter Three

## Stop The World ~ It's Time To Get Off

Grant must have phoned our wonderful friend, Sandra, who lived about thirty minutes away, as she arrived at my doorstep very early that next morning.

I heard her car. I saw her walking up the driveway to our home.

She just looked at me, ashen-faced, and opened her arms.

Neither of us spoke.

She hugged me so tightly and we both cried. I almost collapsed.

Somehow, her standing there with that intense sadness on her lovely face made it all the more real. We cried together.

I don't remember much about the following days. They were a void—a kind of blur. A numb, yet intense pain—that's the only way to describe what I felt at the time. I do know that Grant did not leave Auckland to come and somehow address this. To travel to his wife and confront what was happening face-to-face. All I had was that one phone call.

Could this possibly be the beginning of the end of my marriage?

But ours wasn't the kind of relationship that ended. Was it?

\*\*\*

Sandra's visits during those initial days while I was alone meant the world. She silently cried with me, and just sat with me while I uncontrollably blubbered. Once she said, "I can't believe this is happening," which totally aligned with what I was feeling; I certainly couldn't believe what was happening.

Her being there, just being there, while I sobbed was such a comfort, and I felt that she understood.

Interestingly, all through that period, Sandra never said a disparaging word against Grant, who was her friend, too.

A couple of years later, she became very ill and just before she passed away, she asked me to arrange to have her closest friends visit her. She hesitated for a moment, looked right at me, and said "But not Grant".

That told me a lot.

## A LEARNING MOMENT

### *ACCEPTING HELP*

Many find it hard to ask for help. It's almost as though we have been indoctrinated into believing that seeking help is weak.

It's not.

There's the old saying that a problem shared is a problem halved. I take that to mean being able to say the words to articulate what we are feeling, greatly assists clarity. Spilling out what we are feeling, and doing so in such a way that someone else understands what we are saying, helps us to define our emotions.

Others can't take away our pain or give us the solution, but being heard and fully understood can provide great comfort.

Getting help is the very first step.

If you believe in God, pray for some guidance and support.

If you believe in Guardian Angels, ask for comfort and assistance.

If you believe you walk alone, find a confidant or a counsellor or a friend who will be there.

Seek support.

Ask for help.

Help does not always come in the form of someone giving advice.

Unless someone has literally walked in similar shoes, they can't know what you're feeling.

So, in the spirit of not giving advice, I'm going to give some. I'm kidding...

I wish I had something like this letter to pass to someone wanting to help:

*My dear friend,*

*I am experiencing trauma. My head and my heart are in turmoil and in knots AND in conflict. I feel devastated. I do not know what to do or how I am ever going to get through this.*

*What I need now is for you to just listen.*

*I don't need advice. I will get there in the end.*

*Right now, I just need to be heard and understood. That in itself will give me huge comfort.*

*Also, when I say how horrible my partner/friend is, it's best not to agree. One day we might make up, and in my head, you have now trashed them.*

*There might be times when I contradict myself. I hate him/her! How could they do this to me? Yet in the next breath, I might be sobbing with a broken heart, aching for them, crying that I want them in my life still, and I just don't know how to get them back.*

*It's probably best if you can just buckle up and come for the ride.*

*It's all about me at this moment. If you decide you want to help, I thank you from the bottom of my heart. But I don't need to hear that your work colleague is going through the same thing. I don't care about them.*

*By the way... I probably won't say it right at this moment, but thank you so much for caring enough to just be here for me. It is helping me, and I love you for it.*

# Chapter Four

# Who Said I Have To Decide Now?

Once communication resumed between Grant and me, he made it clear that he wasn't sure of what he wanted. "I love you," he said, "but I have strong feelings for her."

Looking back on that time, I can see this was a probable maneuver where he could have his cake and eat it too, until he had made up his mind. I am sure this 'I love you both' statement was real for him, at the time. While he most probably did love me and all that was 'us', he was most likely not in love with me any longer.

If I were in his shoes, I might have done the same thing. Until I was certain of my feelings, I might try and hold on to both, much like Grant was doing.

Even though I was experiencing huge shock, feeling disbelief, and standing on very unstable ground, I instinctively thought it important to find some semblance of stability and not rush into reactive decisions.

But what to do?

I tend to be quite reactive. Impulsive. I usually trust my first instinct and dive right in.

But this time was different.

I had to pause. To take stock. To make sure I was careful in my decisions and actions as I tried not only to keep our marriage but also to survive this personally and intact.

Just because Grant seemed to be abandoning me, I was not going to instantly abandon the marriage. I was going to fight to the end, even if fighting meant giving him so much space that I lost everything.

> "Never make a major decision when you're down or feeling low."
>
> MY MOTHER

## Chapter Five

# Pause. Don't Rush Into Anything

Another moment that stuck with me was the day we made the decision that we were going to keep this private until there was some certainty. No-one but Sandra knew at that stage.

What if his infatuation with this woman was like a pretty firework—a brightly-colored explosion that quickly faded away?

Yes! That's it. This is a crush he has on her. Lust. Infatuation. A skyrocket that looks and feels amazing, but chances are it could quickly burn out.

I hung on to that tiny light. If this was an 'experience' for him, an 'event', something we 'worked through', something we 'got over' then the fewer people who knew about this, the better.

My daughter (from my first marriage) adored Grant. He was her stepfather and if she knew about his affair, it could have damaged the way she viewed him forever.

I have some warrior women in my life who would never have let me take him back or stay with him. Warrior women who would have surrounded me and fiercely protected me. If they knew.

If he and I somehow managed to work through this—somehow got through and remained together—their view of Grant would have been altered forever if they became aware of his affair.

It's easy to say, "Kick him out!" or "Once a cheater, always a cheater" but when I looked at one of the most significant relationships of my life, I had to be careful how I played this.

However, I had backed myself into a corner where I could not scream and rant, because I didn't want family and close friends to know the details. I did not want to share this horror with anyone in case Grant and I somehow survived this. We had been through a lot, and deep down I hoped we could work through this, too.

I was the deer in the headlights. Frozen and not moving. Intensely hurting. Trying to see how this might be resolved. Trying to hold on to sanity but not being able to tell anyone, not being able to talk about it to anyone. Apart from Sandra.

I constantly felt as though an amateur surgeon was giving me open heart surgery without anesthetic. The unbelievably intense physical pain in my heart was unwavering, unforgiving, torturous... with no relief.

While I had my moments of intense anger with Grant (including smashing several beautiful champagne glasses that were part of a wedding present), I was also aware that Rachel was all sex, newness, and fun, while I must have appeared hurt, betrayed, furious, confused, stale, challenging and confronting.

Plus, I represented the arena where all his guilt lived.

Grant and I had history, but she was the hope, the future, the freshness, and the clean slate.

Still, I made the conscious decision that unless he said he wanted to separate or perhaps even divorce, I would try to somehow get through this with the marriage intact.

At least I had made one decision. And that decision was to do nothing.

I was on a very battered ship, but one that was still afloat. I had taken on water, but I wasn't sinking. Not yet, anyway.

"You cannot see your reflection in boiling water. Similarly, you cannot see the truth in a state of anger. When the water is calm, clarity comes."

MASTERING LAW OF ATTRACTION

**A LEARNING MOMENT**

***THE "T" JUNCTIONS IN THE ROAD OF LIFE***

We come to moments in life that I like to call T-junction. Just the same as real-life highways, each road takes us to separate destinations. We can rarely go back. Our only choice is usually to turn right, or to turn left, knowing each pathway will lead to different outcomes.

Follow your gut when you come to these T-junction moments in your life.

You're the one who makes the choice.

Trust your gut instinct. Trust what you feel to be right.

Try to not be driven by anger, sadness, or even blind enthusiasm.

Follow your own moral compass.

You know deep within yourself what the action or inaction is, that best represents who you really are.

Take the time you need before you decide if left or right will take you to the ideal outcome. Take you to what the ideal outcome is for you.

You could ask yourself, "In five years, will I be happy with myself for the way I chose to handle this?"

# Chapter Six

# Take A Deep Breath

The weeks rolled by as Grant went back and forth, spending time with me at our home, being in Auckland working, and then time with Rachel.

I felt permanently, physically sick.

Rachel.

Who the hell was this woman and what was happening to my world? How much more was going on? How long had this gone on before I found out?

He was open with me about the times he was flying to Australia to be with her, and so I found myself simply waiting.

Waiting. Waiting. Waiting for their flame to burn out and for him to come to his senses.

Part of me felt I had become the passive, silent person in the wings, waiting for a decision from someone else that would affect my life so significantly. But I didn't feel weak. I wrestled with the question of; can I work out how to live with this and give our marriage some hope? I knew if I told him to leave, that decision could well set the ending of our marriage in motion and I wasn't ready to do that.

Because of all we had been through as a couple—all the challenges and struggles, all the good and the bad—I think I would still react the same if I was faced with this scenario today. I would still give such an important decision space and time.

## A LEARNING MOMENT

### *TAKE STOCK, PAUSE, AND SEE IF YOU CAN FORGIVE*

In the movie The Vow, Jessica Lange's character is confronted by her daughter, who is mortified that her mother (Jessica) had stayed with her husband after she found out he had had an affair.

Jessica said; "I chose to forgive him for the one thing he did wrong—for all the things he did right."

Those words resonated with me.

Could I do that? Could I stay with Grant?

If we somehow worked through this, could I continue in our marriage and actually forgive him?

When a person is so significant in our lives, the situation being faced does deserve some time for consideration. It's easy to reactively throw our own bombs on the fire and instantly end the marriage. Maybe some space and time can assist us when sometime later we look back on such events and review how we responded and ultimately behaved.

"The most expensive thing in the world is trust. It can take years to earn and just a matter of seconds to lose."

TINY BUDDHA

# Chapter Seven

# This Is Hell And I Can't Get Out

The physical agony never left me. But suppressing what was happening was starting to really mess with me.

To add salt to the wound, there seemed to be no change.

The days rolled into weeks. One month became two.

One weekend our granddaughter had a birthday, so there was a trip to the zoo. Grant was in Australia. I knew he was spending the weekend with Rachel. He had told my daughter he was going to a conference. Imagine that. My daughter commented that she wondered how Grant's conference was going and I had just shrugged. I was silent. I knew he wasn't at a conference. I knew that right at that moment he was most probably screwing another woman. Oh, God. What a nightmare.

That zoo visit was awful. I did not want to be there. I was quiet, and the last thing I wanted to see were animals housed in cages.

I felt just like them. No space to move.

Every animal looked at me from behind the bars and their vacant stares reflected the trapped angst of my very being.

My beautiful daughter was upset with me on the way home, almost yelling, "What is *wrong* with you?" I replied that I was stressed with work.

She blurted, "I've seen you busy and stressed with business before, and you've never been like this!"

I remained silent.

I was living a lie, and this had to stop.

This situation had gone on long enough and Grant and I decided to send a group message to family and very close friends, saying that we were having some 'marriage trouble' and that we would 'appreciate privacy' while we 'worked through this difficult time'.

This was a huge shock to our close friendship base. They did not know there was someone else; that Grant was in the middle of a full affair. We didn't share the details.

A good friend of ours asked me if Grant was on some sort of medication. "Why would he be having trouble with you," he asked. "You guys are so great together." I just shook my head.

I wasn't exactly lying anymore, but I still suppressed what I really felt.

For some reason, I gave Grant a great deal of rope. Deep down I believed that if I behaved like a screaming nutter, it would make being with her so much easier for him. I felt I had to suppress my real feelings when I was with him. And I felt I had to suppress the full story with friends, because this might still work out between Grant and me. Maybe.

One day, I made my way to a quiet spot on our land and just screamed. While letting out my feelings this way made me feel a little better in that moment, it didn't change a thing as nothing in my new reality was stable.

Let's be real here. There were so many really serious conversations happening between Grant and me. I wasn't just lying there like a doormat. Somehow, I instinctively acted as a stable person in this love triangle. I can imagine that Grant was somewhat torn and that he and Rachel had their 'what are we going to do?' moments, but I was the one who had pushed for this to come out into the open. And so, I was the one living with the consequence. Even though it was so painful, I still held the view that it was better for me to know the state of the cards that I had been dealt than living an illusion.

*Gaynor Morrissey*

# "If you find yourself in hell ... keep going"

**SIR WINSTON CHURCHILL**
...AND MY MOTHER— SHE SAID THIS A LOT!

"We all have an unsuspected reserve of strength inside that emerges when life puts us to the test."

ISABEL ALLENDE

## Chapter Eight

# No Matter How Hard Things Seem, You Can And You Will Get Through It

Finally, the details of the affair came out. While I felt relief that others now understood the full extent of what was going on, I knew I was in for a barrage of questions and judgements.

I don't know what he told his family, but mine rallied around me. While it was comforting, it also unearthed agony as I felt obliged to spill out some details. I had to tell my family and closest friends that my husband was in love with another woman and my marriage might be ending. Saying the words out loud was unbearable; it made the situation an even more sickening reality.

Telling those who loved me and loved Grant became a defining moment. I had been swirling in the chaos as my world disintegrated, but not telling my closest friends and family had been an added agony.

Still, if they had known, their judgements would have been more weight added to my burden and I was already overloaded. A couple of close friends would not have accepted the situation at all and would have been on my case to chuck him out. To end things.

I kept it private so we would be protected from fallout, should his affair blow over. In hindsight, I see that this was not the best move. It was too hard for me. He was the one breaking away from the unit of us, so he should have been made to face the music. But there I was; protecting him.

***

An invisible veil falls over our judgement when we are 'in love'. It's as though we don't want anything to stand in the way of how we view this relationship or new love. This is purely emotional and has no logic to it. But at that moment in time, even though it was Grant who was potentially destroying us, I kept wanting to protect what others thought of him.

I was not going to throw black paint on the canvas that was my marriage, because I was still blindly hanging onto a hope that he and I could resolve things.

> "Love is a verb. Love is what you do... not what you say."

AUTHOR UNKNOWN

# Chapter Nine

# Is Having History Enough?

Grant and I started living together in 1995. He was close to fifty and I was in my early forties. Grant had two children from an earlier marriage, and I had a daughter and step-daughter from my marriage.

We both worked hard and played hard. Financially, it was feasts and famines as we built a life together. Even though there were some very hard moments, there were also many amazing times with parties and overseas trips, and we were always planning fun-filled events. There was always something to look forward to.

As we moved through the years, we decided that when Grant turned sixty, we would semi-retire to a remote area of New Zealand where (at the time) we shared a holiday homestead with others. I would have been in my early fifties by then, and the plan certainly suited me. We would buy the other owners out.

The property was exceptionally rural and raw, and that seemed to suit us.

We both loved the pioneer aspects of life. Hunkering down in the winter. Tending the outdoors in the spring. Feeding the animals and living a basic, more primitive, simplistic life.

The property was a thousand meters above sea level, located in a central North Island, New Zealand location called Ruapehu. The holiday home we shared was the closest homestead to the mighty Mt. Ruapehu. Set in a rural block, the property featured an older house in a majestic setting overlooking a mountain view that constantly changed with the light.

We thrived on the clean, fresh air. The stillness. The beauty of it all. We were going to get out of the city, buy alpacas, get some chickens, ducks, and sheep, and grow our own vegetables. Fresh eggs each morning. Bliss!

And that's what we created.

Grant turned sixty and so we moved out of Auckland, the big city. Both of us found smallish businesses to own and run in the nearest ski-town and we started to build our new life centered on this homestead with some land. We called our home The Lodge.

There we experienced the four seasons in their intensities. Nice dry summers, colorful autumns, snowy winters, and life-bursting springs.

The area was a hotspot for skiing in the winter months, so friends and family would come to our place and we had amazing holidays together. The Lodge was a true gathering place where wonderful memories were created over those years.

Every New Year's Eve, friends from all over New Zealand would come and we would eat, drink, and sing into the night. On New Year's Day, it was traditional for our group to experience some new sort of adventure. New Year's was the height of summer in New Zealand, so we would blast down the steep mountain access road on mountain-bikes, or canoe down the nearest river navigating the rapids.

Great times. Exhilarating stuff. The things that make great memories.

The plan was that we would live on this lifestyle block as we melted into the latter years of our lives. And for about five years, that's what happened.

But the grandchildren started to arrive, and they were in Auckland. This meant fewer visits by family coming to the Lodge and more trips for Grant and me, driving the six hours to Auckland and six hours home again.

There was a strong pull to move back to Auckland.

When we moved south, we came to a quiet rural town which came alive in the ski season, but at that time, not much happened in the other three seasons.

After being there a few years, it felt right to start to divest what we had built in Ruapehu and put our energies into another change—this time, back to where we had come from. We would be able to spend more time with family, and it should prove to be better for us financially.

We decided to move to a beautiful spot, about forty minutes north of Auckland, a magical 'arty-styled' village called Matakana which was a warmer climate, was close to Auckland and had great life-style land sizes for homesteads.

We found the perfect site to start our own business. The plan was that we would wrap things up in Ruapehu, move to Matakana, and I would run our new Matakana business while Grant commuted between the Matakana business and an Auckland venture.

We started the process of selling our Ruapehu interests and putting our homestead on the market. Both of these sales took some time.

Grant started commuting regularly to Auckland and based himself with my daughter, Amber, and her family, staying those few nights a week in their spare room. This was not ideal, but it was to be temporary; only while we were in this transition re-organizing our life.

We found some land for sale at Matakana and started to plan the home we would build. The area was exactly what we both wanted, and this was a great time to build a home that matched our mutual tastes

Grant did a wonderful job getting the Matakana business going, and I stayed in Ruapehu, working through the strategies of our exit. There was a tremendous amount of commuting for both of us, going back and forth between our homestead and Auckland. We were living out of suitcases. Sometimes, I would go to Auckland and other weekends he would come home to the Lodge.

The situation was tolerable because it was a temporary transition, moving toward a well-planned major change. We talked about how this move and our dream home—on a great piece of land and closer to family and friends than Ruapehu—felt like the right thing to do. Grant and I would be working together in our new business venture; it was a change of career for me, but I was okay with that. The move was exciting, and we were both happy with our decision to change. Or so I thought.

# Chapter Ten

# Perfect Ingredients For Disaster

We were busy putting all the bricks in place for our new life. But my new grandson was very sick, and when I commuted to Auckland to be with Grant and the family, my daughter Amber was hoping for some much-needed help. Grant, of course, wanted to go out for dinner since as his wife was back with him. I was torn.

I had no idea that cracks were starting to appear in our marriage, or that they would widen, letting disruption in.

***

When I look back on those months, I see that it was the perfect storm.

We were in a transition. Our world was unstable. We were divesting in one area and creating in another, and there were hours and hours alone in a car for Grant, driving back and forth. Alone with his mobile phone.

Things started to change. I didn't know that another woman was entering the scene in a serious way, but maybe I should have.

He had become self-conscious about his weight. He started exercising. He bought new clothes. He introduced the little blue pill. All of those things were ingredients of a cake stacked with dynamite… I just didn't know it.

The foundations of my life were about to collapse.

# Chapter Eleven

# Facing The Difficult Decisions

Could I somehow ride this out? Work this out... for all that could be destroyed... for all that we had been through and built? Could we possibly continue to have a future? The tormenting questions left me tossing and turning. And besides... I loved this man.

Had I provoked him to act by sending that original phone message demanding to know if he was having an affair? If I hadn't challenged him, would he have continued with the lie until maybe—without the necessity for him to make a decision—his affair might have fizzled out and our marriage could have survived?

But that is not me.

While it was so much more painful for me to know, I did not want to be one of those wives who suppressed her instincts and soldiered on. Any marriage of mine had to have more integrity.

What sort of marriage can face such deceit without affecting the relationship? Lies and cheating like that always impact the relationship. A double life—no matter how small its significance to the cheating spouse—has to have an effect on the marriage.

## Chapter Twelve

# No Change

The utterly insane days that followed his admission flowed into one another. I remained at our homestead, clinging to a life that was in tatters.

I continued to work in our Ruapehu business while waiting for the sale to go through. Each night I went home to the Lodge alone with nothing waiting for me except the scrap of hope that somehow, through this complicated mess, everything would turn out to be all right again.

But things did not look good.

Nothing was stable, apart from my daughters and grandchildren.

My father was dying, and while I was with his doctor being filled in on the full picture of what was happening to him, I found myself sobbing. A good portion of that grief was my chaotic world with Grant, but the doctor read my upset to be solely due to the imminent loss of my father.

She prescribed sleeping pills.

"Just take a half," she said. "It will help you sleep and being rested is a huge advantage to getting through this up-coming loss of your father."

I hadn't taken any form of sleeping medication in my life, so this was somewhat scary. Alone in our bed at night, I tried to sleep, but I found it impossible. I was tortured by mental images of Grant loving Rachel the way he had always loved me. I was drained and exhausted, and being constantly tired affects one's decisions.

I started taking the prescribed half tablet. I was not sure whether this would work as my stomach was in knots, but my eyelids soon felt heavy, and what seemed like a second later, it was morning. At least I could get through the night and then, somewhat rested, tackle the next day.

One day at a time became my new motto.

**A LEARNING MOMENT**

*ONE DAY AT A TIME*

Trying to think too far ahead can wind us up in knots and cause chaos. The implications of a disrupted life can be overwhelming; too much to bear.

If I had contemplated that I would lose almost everything in the early days of this experience, I might have just given up.

In any serious relationship, there are finances, family, friends… all of these strands weave lives together. The thought of unravelling them is huge and devastating. To contemplate the 'what if's' is not a good idea. Taking every day with a 'one day at a time' mentality helps keep things in perspective.

Ideally, we should keep our focus on rest, healthy eating, and comforts, and give ourselves some space.

## Chapter Thirteen

# But What To Do Next?

New Zealand headed into summer and into the southern hemisphere's Christmas and summer holidays.

Nothing had changed. Grant was still creating the circus of time with Rachel, then time with me.

One day while he was in Australia with Rachel, Grant phoned me and said that he was coming home and would like us to try again. I was euphoric.

I asked him if Rachel knew. He said no. That should have been an indicator.

He came back to New Zealand, but there was no real attempt to reconcile.

Even though he was expressing that he was still in doubt, I now see that in reality, he had already gone.

Whatever the reasons were behind that apparent flicker of doubt in his world no longer mattered.

Now it appeared as though he was trying to be faithful to Rachel, not me.

***

The timing of him possibly ending our marriage seemed so bloody unfair.

Our kids were no longer teenagers. My parents had both passed. I was now out of menopause.

This was supposed to be *our* time, the time for us where we were technically free.

And he was considering leaving?

# Chapter Fourteen

# The Night Of The Real Separation

As usual, when I visited Auckland, we always stayed at my daughter's. In the same room and in the same bed, although we were no longer intimate. During one of those visits, Grant suggested that we go out to dinner at one of our favorite restaurants, a popular Steak House in the central city. This was a good sign; a night out together.

We placed our usual order, with our usual wine. The food arrived, and it looked wonderful.

I was about to start eating when Grant announced out of the blue that he would like a separation. Not a formal, legal separation, but some time apart so he could 'get some clarity'.

I choked. I stood. I started to cry. As I ran out of the restaurant and crossed the road to get to my car, he followed me and called my name.

My heart skipped a beat. My breath stuck in my throat, and I thought, this could be like a movie… I hoped to hear, "My darling, forgive me. That was a mistake to say that… I don't want to lose you… I don't want to lose us."

Instead, he said, "You've left your wallet on the table."

I grabbed the wallet and headed to my car. Paying the parking fee was a blur, heading on the motorway back to my daughter's home was a blur.

He was in his car, I was in mine, and we were heading to the same house. To the same room.

When I arrived, I blurted out to my poor daughter that we were now really separating.

That night, I slept apart from him. In all the years we were together, we had never slept apart when we were in the same location.

The next day was intensely painful, and although I cried inconsolably, I somehow managed to pack and head back to the Lodge.

The implosion which was my life was getting worse, not better.

I phoned my dear Canadian friend, Wendy. Somehow telling my closest friend that my marriage was in serious trouble was a confirmation in my head. Telling her that Grant was in the process of leaving me and that he had asked for a separation, made the situation I was in a solid and horrible reality.

"Wendy," I said, "I can't be here for the summer. Can I come to you?"

No hesitation. "Of course."

I began planning to go to Canada for at least a few weeks.

From New Zealand, Canada was halfway around the world. But at least I had a plan: to get out of this situation and into the loving protection of my dearest friend, to try and make sense of my world, because I was out of control.

I told Grant I was heading to Canada. The day of my departure, he asked to meet me and had brought me a gift; expensive headsets for the trip. He drove me to where my car was parked and as I went to get into my vehicle, he stopped me; then he took my face in both hands, and kissed me. It was one of the best kisses he had ever given me. It was so warm and tender and he was so present.

I had no idea if that would be our very last kiss. No idea of how this was all going to pan out. All I knew was that I loved him. That he was with another woman and that I had to protect myself.

## Chapter Fifteen

# Time To Take Stock

I arrived in Ontario on Christmas Eve. The Canadian winter really laid on the cold and the snow. A huge bonus for me was that the homes were all lit up with Christmas lights. It was a beautiful sight to behold, with the snow reflecting lights. A few hours earlier I had been in the midst of our New Zealand summer, and the concept of a white Christmas was so different for me.

Wendy and her husband Jim, opened up their cozy home to me and I found myself in a very safe port in my storm. Some may think I was running from my problem by heading to Canada. The reality was that I needed to have some form of safety net. Wendy was that net.

I spent hours just crying—sobbing actually—with Wendy just listening.

The days melted into each other.

"This is what a broken heart looks like," the wise and beautiful Wendy gently said... "But you need to know that it will heal."

I did not believe her.

Wendy worked from their home in a separate downstairs apartment, so I had many hours to myself.

Every morning after breakfast, I bundled up in a winter coat and warm boots and went for a robust walk. Upon my return, I took a shower and dressed properly, with full make-up and perfume—even if we were not going out.

Somehow, I knew that living in UGG boots and sloppy clothes, ignoring my grooming, would take me down a dark rabbit hole.

I stuck to a self-imposed regular pattern. Looking back, I can see how incredibly important that daily routine was.

Getting up at the same time every single day, having breakfast, cleaning the kitchen, shoveling the sidewalk snow, and collecting the firewood in from the outside stack helped keep my mind occupied. I was in the depth of a real Canadian winter, and these daily routines were part of survival.

Repeating this same pattern everyday represented some stability.

I instinctively knew I had to put one foot in front of the other. I had to get through each day, and only each single day. Thinking of anything beyond that was not possible. I didn't have any idea in which direction my world was headed.

"Sometimes" said the horse "Sometimes what?" asked the boy. "Sometimes just getting up and carrying on is brave and magnificent."

THE BOY, THE MOLE, THE FOX AND THE HORSE
CHARLIE MACKESY

## Chapter Sixteen

# Am I Brave Enough To Face The Reality?

Being ten thousand miles away from home gave me space, and I started to think that maybe Grant was missing me. This became my new fantasy.

Of course, he would be missing me! It was summer in New Zealand and that was when we played. Off to the beach, camping, boating, skiing, and nights of beach dinners and wine. Relaxation, fun, singing, laughter, loving. That was what we did.

I went into the bank account and checked the spending, and my world spun all over again as I saw from the charges that he was taking Rachel to all the places he and I had gone. All the places that we usually go. She was in New Zealand and he was taking her everywhere that had been 'ours'.

I couldn't believe it.

Wendy's husband Jim shook his head, not comprehending why I was torturing myself this way by looking at these bank charges with each betrayal stacking on top of the last. In my mind, this action somehow made me face the reality of what was happening, not the fantasy of how I thought it might be.

Looking at this spending was a hard thing to do. I would see what they were doing, and I felt like vomiting. Literally. My heart wasn't healing, it was breaking all the more. But I had to face the reality of the situation, no matter how much I wanted to run away.

Was my being away giving him a clean space to develop his new relationship? Perhaps. But my decision to be in Canada was because getting away was the right thing for *me*. I didn't go there in an attempt to make him miss me, or because spending more day-to-day time with Rachel might make him rethink his life and possibly come back to me. I went away to protect myself.

I don't look on it so much as a gamble. If my putting pressure on him resulted in him staying, then he may well have stayed, but instinctively I thought that any deviation of 'us' (i.e., his affair) had to play out rather than be suppressed.

A gamble? Yes.

But the bottom line was that I would rather be the woman he thought about sometimes, than the one with him wondering who he might be thinking about.

"Face what actually is.

If you face the reality—truly face it head on—then at least you know what you are dealing with, with no illusions.

This is the most painful way to do it, but, in the long run, you will find that it was the quickest way to genuinely get through, and to come out the other side."

GAYNOR

## Chapter Seventeen

# Confrontation Time

I had been away from my home in New Zealand for about three weeks when my neighbor, who was house-sitting and caring for our dog, mentioned in one of our regular calls that Grant had been down to The Lodge to collect the tents and camping equipment.

Oh no… Rachel's still there in New Zealand with him and they're going camping! That's our place. That's what he and I do!

I rang him and said that if he was making plans with Rachel, he needed to face that he and I were really over. I was not going to be the one that ended the marriage. I still wanted the marriage, and if it was going to end, *he* had to end it.

His reply? "I am making plans with her."

"That's it then," I said with a flat, deadened voice, and I hung up.

I was outside on a veranda looking at the neighbors' twinkly house lights. I just stood there for a moment, silent and still. Then I took a deep breath before I went back inside and told my Canadian friends, "This is the moment my marriage ended."

Oh, the grief… the agony… as deep down a part of me had hung on to the tiny hope that one day, I would be receiving a call from him where he put me first, wanted to repair; wanted to still have our marriage. But now with the news that Grant and Rachel were making plans for their future, I knew a reconciliation was not going to happen.

*\*\*\**

During these weeks in Canada, I met Wendy's friend, Red, and had a couple of counselling sessions with him. He was so patient while I sobbed and blurted my heart out.

'But he used to call me so many times in a day,' I cried. 'He's the one I talk to about everything.' In our time together, we had spoken millions of words and shared thoughts, and now the communication had been brutally cut.

Is that it? The life we'd built just ends?

Red said, "So what do you want to talk to him about?" (I couldn't readily answer that one). "If you could talk to him, would you want to raise the subject of what has happened?"

He went on to say. "He picked up the vase that was your marriage and smashed it… and you're running around trying to collect all the pieces to put it back together again… and even if you can, haven't you just got a cracked vase?"

And the final words… "Maybe one day you will think that by leaving you, he gave you the greatest gift of all."

Oh, how could this person misunderstand this situation so? By leaving me, Grant is giving me a gift…. A *gift*?

Maybe Red was piecing together the words I was blubbering and concluding that my being with Grant, or 'winning' him back, was not going to be the best outcome for *me*. At the time, I did not see that as a possibility. How could I be better off without him?

It's always interesting that another person who is not emotionally involved can see the picture so clearly. I couldn't. My viewpoint was clouded with so many conflicting emotions. I professed that I loved Grant. I kept saying that we had built this life together and that we had a great bond. But my dearest friends could see that my being with Grant was not the best for me. They are such good friends that they gave me the space to realize this for myself. I would have hated anyone who trashed him at that time.

Counsellor Red could see. He was not emotionally involved as I was. His guidance to me was *for* me and there were no suggestions on how I could repair my marriage. He could clearly see that it was not repairable.

"You are braver than you believe, stronger than you seem, smarter than you think, and loved more than you know."

AA MILNE

## Chapter Eighteen

## Retreat ~ Regroup

The Canadian days turned into weeks as I followed my new strict routine. Always get out of bed. Always. Never lie in. Eat good food, take a walk. Then get fully dressed, do domestic tasks.

Slowly, I started thinking that maybe, things weren't going to get worse. Very, very slowly I started preparing to get back into life.

Friends now knew we were really separated, and my wonderful long-term friend, Vicki, sent me a daily text from New Zealand, along the lines of 'You are loved', 'It will all turn out alright', and 'know that we love you'. Every single day a text of comfort came to me from her, and that went on for weeks. I don't think she will ever fully appreciate how heart—warming those texts were in the cold desert I found myself in.

Wendy assured me that I could stay with them for as long as I liked, and I was grateful for that too. But I had family and grandchildren at home in New Zealand, and there had to come a time when I would go back.

I had to.

But I had no home to go back to as our Lodge was being sold. Not only did I have no place to live, but I had no job, because we were still in the process of selling our Ruapehu business interests, and the plan had been that I was supposed to work in our Matakana business with Grant. He did suggest that. Even though he was planning a new life with Rachel, he suggested to me that I go through with our plans and work together with him in our new business.

I was starting to wonder what planet he was living on.

He was separated from me, openly wining and dining his new woman, and he thought I might be okay working in the business venture that was to be his and mine? At times, that man made me shake my head in disbelief.

There are no rules when it comes to healing…

You move to your own timeline.

Grief is heavy… so give yourself the space to live in it for its time.

…but don't make it your new home.

GAYNOR

*Gaynor Morrissey*

"Self-care isn't just drinking water and going to sleep early.

Self-care is taking a break when things become overwhelming.

Saying 'no' to things you do not want to do.

Allowing yourself to cry.

Asking for help from those around you.

Doing things that make you happy."

THEDAILYREMINDERS

## Chapter Nineteen

## Maybe There Is Hope

Those weeks in Canada were the very best thing I could have possibly done for myself.

Being with Wendy gave me space, time, and safe surroundings to work through the shock and take stock. Her wisdom and love were both unconditional and full.

It sounds so odd, but deep down within me, while I was starting on the healing process, I still had the thought that maybe when I got back to New Zealand, Grant would be ready to see if we could work this through after all. We had so much history. So much of our lives we had shared.

Even though he was now spending more time with Rachel, and we were 'separated', he and I had not been apart for any real length of time until now. Maybe there was a glimmer of hope. Maybe their rocket was starting to fade. Maybe life without me was not all that wonderful.

The power of hope has a strong pull.

While I was so wounded that I was figuratively bleeding from every orifice, I somehow managed to keep getting up again like a Rocky movie. Somehow, I clung to grains of hope that he and I might still make it.

The heart and the head surely live in different realities.

## Chapter Twenty

# It Gets Real

One evening, I took my vitamins and a half sleeping tablet as usual. After a short Kindle read, I promptly drifted off to sleep.

At about one a.m. I woke with a start, with a very real thought that had brought me from deep sleep to a state of being awake in an instant, 'I bet he had an earlier affair,' or at least an encounter. Maybe several encounters, several affairs.

Trust your instincts, I thought. If there was another affair, who was it with?

The name flashed in neon lights instantly in front of me... Julie.

I grabbed my laptop and Googled. Found her and lifted the phone to ring her.

I had not planned what to say. I just knew I had to phone her immediately.

She remembered me; she knew Grant and I had separated.

"But before I decide what I am going to do, there is something I need to know about you and Grant," I blurted out. Her response was asking me if I could call her back in about an hour.

Call her back? WTF!

So, picture this. It's the middle of the night where I am in Canada. I had taken that sleeping tablet earlier, and now I was in the position where I needed to call this person back in an hour.

I had to set my alarm to phone a woman half way across the planet, to ask her if she had slept with my husband. How bizarre is that! Rather hilarious, when you think about it. When I told Wendy about this over breakfast, we both looked at each other and started to laugh at the absurdity of it and from then on, she would take my mobile and laptop from me before I went to bed—like a controlling mother.

So there I was in a really deep drug-induced sleep when the alarm went off, and for a moment I couldn't figure out why the alarm was sounding.

I remembered, sat up, and hit Redial.

It kept ringing (I started to think she was avoiding the call).

"I'm appealing to the sisterhood (I said). I need you to be honest with me, woman-to-woman. I really need to know. Did you have an affair with Grant?"

With no hesitation, she responded with a 'yes' and when I questioned for how long, she added "for several weeks" (he had been sleeping with someone else for *weeks*!).

"I like married men," she said. "I have my fun, but I always give them back."

I felt dirty.

I thanked her for being honest. (*I thanked her*)!

I was about to hang up when she hesitated and asked if she could send me something—a paper on human behavior that was part of her current studies. "Fine," I said. "Send me anything."

The next morning, I received an email with a document commenting about repetitive behavior. Basically, it was saying a leopard doesn't change its spots. The 'sisterhood' was trying to tell me that this would happen again.

I had instincts about Julie. Actually, I had felt the stomach bells ringing about three or four other women over the years, but I had dismissed the feelings. But now I knew my instinct about Rachel was right, and my instinct about Julie was right. I no longer cared to know about any others. What was the point?

The leopard had spots.

"The people you meet are either reflections of a repeated cycle or guides towards a new start. Notice the difference."

TINY BUDDHA

"When you finally learn that a person's behavior has more to do with their internal struggle than it ever did with you, you learn grace."

ALISON AARS

## Chapter Twenty-One

# I Finally See The Pattern

As I look back on these moments—these events, these pockets of happenings—I can clearly see in hindsight that they were all lining up to guide me. Droplets of knowledge or random realizations pushed me along the path of facing the reality of my marriage.

It wasn't good.

Had it ever been good? I mean good? Or were we just living in the routine of so many years together?

No outsider can get into a tight marriage. There have to be cracks before they can slip in.

I think, in hindsight, that I knew there were cracks but I ignored them.

"Sometimes people leave because they aren't ready to love.

Sometimes they leave because they are chasing a feeling and don't know how to find it within themselves.

Sometimes they leave because they have to go in order to grow.

Sometimes they leave because they don't yet know who they are.

Sometimes people just leave, and it doesn't always mean something about you, your worth or how loveable you are.

Let them go."

VICTORIA ERIKSON

# Chapter Twenty-Two

# Finally Facing The Reality

I had to face the fact that I was not going back to repair my marriage. I was heading back to New Zealand to start rebuilding my life.

Sooner or later, I had to go home, and I would have to rebuild almost every facet of my life from scratch, with minimal resources—especially financial resources. I was broke and aged fifty-eight, which is not a good age to start over.

Starting again takes strength, and I was sapped of all energy.

How was I possibly going to face moving from our home—and where to?

How was I to build a new life and with what? And where? And how?

How was I going to get a job? I needed to get a job, because I was certainly not going to work with Grant in the Matakana business. But I hadn't applied for a job since I was eighteen. Even though I had worked all my life, it was in partnerships and I had been self-employed and I hadn't worked for an employer.

My future looked bleak.

But those who loved me had wholeheartedly surrounded me with warmth and calmness, and deep down I started to feel that maybe I was going to be okay after all.

Still, the idea that I had to rebuild almost all components of my life was hard to face. I had no reserves. Any build-back was going to be on slim foundations, and I was almost out of gas.

The wonderful, beautiful, loving Wendy assured me I could stay with her in Canada for as long as I needed to, but I knew I had to face my new life at some point. I will be forever grateful for the wonderful Wendy and Jim for providing me with that cushion of sanity and safety. But after three months away, it was time to return to New Zealand.

I knew I wasn't going back to anything solid. There was the love from my family and closest friends, but I had no picture of my future. No certainty.

My time in Canada was not *running* from the truth. Rather, it was a safe space for me to face the honest truth of my world and to recuperate… to take a breath… to take stock of the reality of all that had happened and all that I had to now face.

*Gaynor Morrissey*

"One day you'll look back and realize how hard it was, and just how well you did."

THE BOY, THE MOLE, THE FOX AND THE HORSE
CHARLIE MACKESY

"You will never speak to anyone more than you speak to yourself in your head. Be kind to yourself."

TINY BUDDHA

## A LEARNING MOMENT

### *SELF-PROTECTION*

When there is such loss, it is important that we self-protect. On an airplane, the instructions are to put our own oxygen mask on first before caring for others. Removing myself gave me a chance at self-protection, of trying to stabilize myself when things were so chaotic. I have never looked back on the decision to go away to Canada, for that time, with any regret. Quite the opposite. I know deep down that it saved my sanity.

Self-protection is self-care. This is not a strategy; it's more of a tool.

Creating some distance from the chaos does not mean that you have to travel half-way around the world though.

To 'protect' ourselves can be as simple as not engaging in endless and painful phone calls with the former partner for a while. Creating some space to allow ourselves to get some clarity on what it is that we genuinely want. That's part of self-care.

Many break-ups come with an element of pain even when we are the ones causing the break-up.

The ending of a relationship is, in effect, the death of that relationship and so there is some loss to whatever degree.

And loss needs to be felt for its time.

"Take a deep breath. No matter how hard things seem right now, you can and you will get through it."

@MELTBLOGS

*Gaynor Morrissey*

# "Every storm runs out of rain."

MAYA ANGELOU

## Chapter Twenty-Three

# Following My Moral Compass

I left Canada on March 31st and came home to the beginnings of the New Zealand Autumn.

Our home by the mountain still had to be sold, and Grant was working full time in Auckland, so I headed to the Lodge and gave myself a target of three months. Twelve weeks to pack up the life that we had built over all those years, move to somewhere, find a place to live, and get a job. Money was tight for me, but I wasn't going anywhere, so there was nothing to spend it on.

I started to pack up my tattered world.

There were moments when the grief of this process took me by surprise. Not so long ago, I had visualized that packing up this home would be full of joy as we would be moving to our new life in Matakana.

Even though I was by myself doing this, I was relieved that I was doing this on my own, without Grant being there. I could not have faced that.

After many days of exhaustive and sometimes painful sorting, I had packed all of my possessions in a large shipping container I had arranged to be placed on our land until the property sold, since I had no place to move my things to. Where was I going to live?

Once all of my stuff was packed, I could have easily gotten into my car at that moment and headed to my daughter's home in Auckland, leaving Grant's personal things for him to sort. But I decided to handle the whole homestead's possessions; my stuff, Grant's belongings, and what was going to be left to go with the sale of the property.

So, I turned my attention to Grant's personal things.

This was a "T-junction" moment for me.

How was I going to treat his things?

Make a nice bonfire in the yard? Or be the bigger person?

The bonfire was tempting. I'm no saint, and maybe he deserved it. His actions had destroyed my life so I could have destroyed his things.

But I bubble-wrapped, boxed, and labelled all of Grant's possessions and had them stacked safely on wooden pallets waiting to be collected. I handled his possessions with care.

I feel an inner sense of peace that despite the way I'd been treated, I chose to deal with things with grace. That was a decision I made for *me*, not for anyone else. I didn't care how Grant viewed it.

Ironically, the decision ended up being my gift to me; looking back, I feel proud of myself and how I behaved.

Let's be clear. My decision at that time as to how I was going to treat his things might not work for everyone. There is a huge satisfaction being able to finally express the hurt and pain by cutting up clothes or selling their treasured possessions. Releasing the fury can be a way of 'getting back' and I know it works for many people.

But in this instance, and at that time, destruction was not the way I handled it. We're all different and we do what feels right for us at the time.

I left furniture and kitchenware with the property, including the beautiful baby—grand piano that had been a gift from Grant. But where the hell was I going to put that? I had no idea where I was going to live but I knew that it could not be in a space that had room for a baby-grand.

I remember the day I came home to that beautiful piano. I loved to play and loved Grant all the more for knowing what that special gift would mean to me. He used to do wonderful things like that. But he was also a cheater.

"You are always responsible for how you act. No matter how you feel."

ROBERT TEW

## Chapter Twenty-Four

## First Steps Of The Rebuild

The sale of the Lodge finally went through but after paying off the mortgage and other loans, there wasn't much money left over. Certainly not enough for me to have any real future financial security. The business sold too and again, there was a minimal return because the need to sell quickly meant we had to accept lower offers.

Moving back to Auckland and close to family seemed to be the only option for me.

A wonderful friend, Colleen, said that she might know somewhere for me to live. When I next went to Auckland, I checked this out, but it was not right for me. Things looked grim. I left that viewing feeling very low.

Heading back to my daughter's house, I had to drive past the building where Grant worked.

I was stopped at the lights and as I looked across, I could see Grant and his colleagues sitting outside their workplace, in the sun, drinking coffee. Grant must have heard something funny; he started to laugh and in his usual fashion, threw his head back in an open laugh. He was calm and happy. He looked like he didn't have a care in the world.

I had seen and heard that laugh a million times. But here I was, lost and frightened, feeling incredibly sad, and he was surrounded by colleagues and laughing. He was happy!

He didn't see me. The lights turned green, and I moved on, my stomach in an aching knot, my heart in pain, and my head in chaos.

***

There is no such thing as alimony in New Zealand. If a marriage falls apart, then ultimately the net assets are split, but there is no spousal support. None. Nada. Zip.

I needed a job.

I contacted an acquaintance who was well—connected in the Auckland business—world and asked for a meeting, hoping he could give me leads toward finding a job. He gave me three contacts and said that he would phone them and recommend me.

One contact was for a dynamic woman who had started an amazing fundraising platform which was taking New Zealand by storm. She agreed to meet me over a coffee, and I gave her my pitch.

"I'm not after a job with you, but here's my background and this is what I am looking for and if you know of anyone..."

This conversation resulted in this woman and her husband inviting me to look after their businesses for a few weeks while they were in Europe. I came to Auckland, stayed with Amber and the family, and went to work. For the first time in more than thirty years, I worked for a boss.

The routine gave me a sense of stability, but I knew I had to get a real job. I also couldn't live with family permanently.

The owners rang from Europe and asked me to stay on, so I did. An apartment which was perfect for me fell into my lap. It was centrally located, right by live music and cafes and away from the area of Auckland where Grant was. New faces. New people.

I was independent, and while still aching in my heart and soul, at least I had made a fresh start in a new environment.

It took some effort to garner the courage to make the initial calls to try and find work, but I had pushed myself. I had to.

The job realistically fell into my lap, and my great-yet-affordable apartment just appeared. There really wasn't a lot of effort to finding either of them. I was grateful that these two bricks of my new life were now in place.

## A LEARNING MOMENT

### *FIRST STEPS*

Reaching the stage of trying to find somewhere to live or a job to provide income is so important. If that doesn't happen, it becomes a dwindling spiral.

Reach out to friends and colleagues. Spread the word that you need some help. Obtain some professional assistance with creating a work experience profile if you have to. At this point, you have to pull up your socks and just do it.

The foundation of independence lies in taking the steps required to become independent.

But don't beat yourself up if it doesn't all happen on the first day. It can take time, and that's okay as long as you make some form of effort every single day. Sometimes it's a good idea to look at making a change. Get a new haircut. Change your makeup. Do something different for a different result. Then move on to working on a CV and start to promote yourself.

This is a time to rely on friends. Follow up on every single offer of help.

Take the steps. The first ones are hard. Forging out to try and find somewhere to live and work adds to the reality that life has changed. But each step, each phone call, each grain of effort is an ingredient in the start of self—repair.

> As I write this, I can feel again how frightened I was. It took every bit of my reserve to put one foot in front of the other every day, when I had such a heavy heart. But somehow, we have to believe that we will make it through.

# Chapter Twenty-Five

# Careful With The Spending!

The weeks rolled by.

I went on a spending spree. I needed to get furnishing for my apartment, everything from a new bed to a washing machine and dryer, and TV. All I had was my credit cards and a need.

The positive side was that I was getting pleasure from buying the things that I wanted. I chose décor that suited me. Our earlier homes had the masculine feel that Grant wanted. At the time, I was okay with that. But this shopping was fun. I loved putting my taste, my stamp, on my own surroundings.

The negative side was that I was maxing my credit cards. The pleasure of buying new things could easily become a form of replacement addiction. I needed furniture, but I also went overboard with clothes and shoes.

At the time, it didn't seem to matter, and it gave me some temporary happiness. Luckily, I was able to rein myself in and once I had the basics, I knew it was time to stop spending.

But I had to work hard on getting the card debt handled.

My car crapped out; it literally stopped. So, I needed another.

I went to the same dealer where Grant and I had purchased vehicles over the years. I test-drove and made the decision. Financially, this was going to be tight, but a newer, more reliable car gave me some comfort and pleasure, and I justified the purchase to myself by saying that I deserved it.

Let's be real. This purchase was way above what I should have gone for financially. I am not sure why I extended myself the way that I did. Looking back, I think it was because I needed something really nice in my life. I wanted to feel good every time I got into this car. It was a stupid financial decision but it gave me such joy and I needed some happiness in my life right then.

The salesman took me through syncing my mobile phone through Blue-tooth. "Okay," he said. "Let me show you how this works." He whizzed through the names stored. He knew Grant but did not know that we were no longer together, and he looked at me, smiled and said, "Okay, here we go! Let's phone this guy."

But had renamed Grant's contact name as Grant-Bastard, to remind myself that when he called me, I was not to be taken in by any charming voice. This was not my man; this was the man who had blown my world apart.

The salesman saw the wording. His eyes grew wider. He said nothing; I said nothing. He moved on to another name and dialed.

I can only imagine the conversation in the sales staff room after I left...

\*\*\*

There are moments when you make the purchase and say to yourself, "I deserve it," but you also need to keep to your budget, or this can become a new problem.

I quickly realized that things were out of control. Retail therapy was my new drug. My new comfort. I was hooked.

Fortunately, I could see that I was in a bad place. It hit me in the face when my fortnightly pay went to car payments, rent, food, and credit card minimums. I was being charged too much interest each month, and I couldn't see how this could reverse.

I asked for help. The spending had to stop. Buying 'stuff' gave me comfort, but I was trying to fill an emptiness. I appeased myself by saying that at least my addiction was not drugs, drinking, gambling, or new relationships. My enemy was the credit cards.

Luckily, my wonderful stepdaughter, Denise, is very good with money, and I turned to her. Her advice was to go cold turkey; to cut up all credit cards. While the advice made me shake, I did it— apart from one card which I froze in an ice cube. That card was my final safety net, my security blanket. I thought that if I was really stuck, all I had to do was to take it out of the freezer and wait for it to thaw.

Over the next months, the card balances slowly reduced. At least the debt didn't increase with new purchases.

I began to food shop differently. I was focused on items that could stretch to two or three meals. I had to make this change.

Denise had me write down my income, my expenses, and my longer-term debt (the cards and the car). With some help, I created a workable budget and stuck with it. It's like a health plan that only works if we stick at it.

Occasionally, I came across the most wonderful things that I wanted to buy. Funny how when we have some cash in our pockets, these great things are hard to find. Make the decision not to spend, and there they are, in the display windows and on sale!

Life felt so unfair. Here I was with a shell-shocked heart and I couldn't even get a new coat to comfort me.

# Chapter Twenty-Six

# What About Friends And Family?

Over the next months, I had a routine to my day. I had a job, a nice new car, and an apartment, but I was empty inside.

The great friends who were couples, people we had socialized with over many years, slowly drifted away. The circle we had mixed in was melting.

I understand how difficult it can be for friends when a couple split.

Who do you choose? Which side are you on? I didn't want any choosing to happen. I didn't even want to talk about Grant. I just wanted some company.

I knew this part of my life was over. Even if somehow Grant and I could get back, the bonds that tied these wonderful friendships over the years were tarnished. Some had been cut and things would not be the same. Could not be the same.

Grant had chosen new excitement over cherished history. And I was history. Even though I knew this to be a fact and even though I knew that he was building a new life, every single time my phone rang, my heart skipped a beat thinking that maybe that was him calling to try and reconcile. That went on for a year. *One whole year.* Reflecting on that, I know that this was because Grant had so much credit in the bank of 'us', and while it had recently been robbed, some of that metaphorical credit was still there.

Part of me ached for what had been, but at the same time, another part was so hurt by his cavalier behavior. Perhaps his heart and head knew he was distracted and he was putting us to a test while we were still together, without me knowing anything about it.

But if the normal married day-to-day with me was not what he wanted, then I was ultimately going to be better off if it ended. I just didn't think so at the time.

This process of trying to get through the pain of the loss and, at the same time, trying to build a path that I hadn't planned on creating was hard. The idea of a new home for Grant and I and a new business working with Grant, had evaporated.

...and gone was the Matakana dream.

The wider family tree had blown apart, too. There was his side of the family with children and relatives, and there was mine. I lost all of the extended family. While his side of our large family were shocked at our breakup, they were Grant's family, and some of them did not contact me at all.

The double or triple whammy of losing friends and family seems so unfair particularly where we perceive ourselves as the victim—the one who did no wrong. But in most divorces, this is the price you pay. I really loved some of his family, and their loss only added to my grief. But to genuinely start again—to fully create a new life—sometimes we need to let these folks drift away.

New doors do open. New friendships. New relationships. But at the time of loss, it does not look as if it could ever happen.

I appreciated it when a friend empathized with what I was going through. I have to say, though, that there were so many people that were quite close to Grant and me and yet they never mentioned that they knew that we had split up. It's almost like they hold the view that some things are best left unsaid.

**A LEARNING MOMENT**

***THE AWKWARDNESS – WHAT TO SAY?***

Some friends feel so uncomfortable with separations or divorces that there's avoidance and awkwardness in conversations. They don't mention that they met up with the former spouse or that they ran into him/her.

Some people will cross the street rather than face us because they feel so uncomfortable and unsure about what to say. Others phone straight away and address the reality by expressing that they are sorry for our loss.

The avoiders are not wrong. They are just unsure and uncomfortable. Sometimes their lack of communication is because they don't want to upset the grieving person by mentioning it. There are a couple of members of Grant's family who I never heard from again. I found that to be very strange. I think some lies got in there somehow and maybe they saw me differently. I will never know.

I believe that it's best to get the elephant out of the room and make the call and offer support, or simply acknowledge that you are aware of what has happened and that you were sorry to hear about it.

Make the call. Go visit the person if you can. Say some words. And then it's done. I have been on both ends of this and I can say that receiving communication from someone after a loss means so much. I used to send sympathy cards to friends and acquaintances when I learned of a death in their family and simply popped the card in the post. When my mother passed away, and after a little bit of time, I remember reading all of the messages the family received and felt a deep sense of gratitude. I had not realized how warmly kind gestures are received until I was on the receiving end.

## Chapter Twenty-Seven

# His Life Pattern Was There For Me To See – But I Was Blind

Grant had a history. Basically, his love life had consisted of moving from one woman to the next. He never had a period of time where he was on his own.

He loved women. And women loved him.

But when he and I got together, I had fallen for his words: "You are the love of my life", and "No-one knows me the way you know me", and "No-one has loved you as much as I love you."

We were older when we married, and because we seemed to be such a good match, I did not contemplate that he would have affairs or leave me.

His life pattern was laid out in front of me and well-known to me, but I had fallen for the classic: This time it will be different for him.

Love is blind.

His pattern of 'woman, home, dog, affair, leave' had repeated so much in his past and became glaringly obvious again when I came to learn that Grant had moved to Australia and was living with

Rachel. Apparently, they purchased a new home together—in a lifestyle block, with alpacas and a dog. Just as we had. He had replicated the life but changed the woman. Go figure.

The pattern that was his life vividly flashed before me like a neon sign flashing. He was living a pattern and will continue to do so. Repeat. Repeat. Repeat.

Love sure is blind.

The idea that 'this time it will be different' didn't stand a chance. How blind was I to think that there was a hope in hell of our time being any different?

I now see patterns in people and the way they have lived and are living their lives. Patterns of behavior. Patterns in lives.

Once I was on my own, I spent some time looking internally at my own patterns of behavior and some of it wasn't all that pretty. Even though I am a reasonably strong woman, I fell (in both of my marriages) into a behavior that did not always voice what I wanted. It felt easier to bend to what he wanted. Don't get me wrong, I was not subservient, but I see in hindsight that I did jump when called, especially with Grant. During the initial love-bombing I received, he was so very grateful and appreciative of every little thing I did to make his life easier. I see now that he was setting the foundations of how things were going to be. Our pattern had begun.

I look back and reflect that he was not so wonderful at doing things to make my life easier. While he was still verbally appreciative of me, of every meal, of having clothes cleaned and cared for, my planning my days around his schedule, I now see hindsight moments that he did not show the respect for me as his wife that he should have. But here's the thing. I tolerated that. I shake my head when I think back and realized that I tolerated things. It was so subtle—the appearance of these red flags and patterns—that I wasn't fully conscious of them and did not raise them with him at the time they were happening.

I was whole-heartedly in the marriage; I was fully committed and did not create unhappiness or fights. But I also did not stick up for myself to the level I should have.

Hindsight is twenty-twenty and I now see that there was an imbalance in our supportive actions. Oh yes, we had wonderful times, but those wonderful times suited Grant's wants. I don't think we did much at all that Grant participated in that did not really suit him, and that he ended up coming along because it suited me. Hardly ever.

I now see that for so long, deep down, I felt that I was 'sacrificing'. Sacrificing my energies and my attention, which is okay to do but not the best when there is not much coming back from the other side.

Don't get me wrong. Grant created great experiences and was always planning the next thing to do or the next place to go for a holiday and I usually enjoyed most of these activities. But. And there is a 'but'. Thinking about our life together, I recall some of my suggestions being steered more towards something that suited him. I did not see this very clearly at the time.

# Chapter Twenty-Eight

# What Happened? I Thought Things Were Good

One of my first thoughts when the breakup happened, was about how *I* could change. How could I fix things to suit him better?

"I should have given him more attention."

"Maybe I shouldn't have prioritized our grandchildren."

"When was the last time I made an effort to make my partner feel special?"

If I made changes, then that might hold him in the marriage?

In any marriage there are times when the balance gets out of whack, and then somehow seems to self-correct. There are times when energy is weighted more with one person, then it swings back to the other person. Sometimes one partner needs more attention or resources. This kind of give-and-take happens in all relationships.

But if I had to make changes to me, in the hope that a partner would then decide to stay with me, I didn't want it. That realization was a biggie for me.

***

This story makes him out to be a villain, but he was actually a rather amazing man. A fully masculine man. A very capable man. A leader. A man's man (and, unfortunately, a women's man).

I have to refer to him in the past as that is how I mainly view him. I hope he still has his positive traits, because they were great.

Capable, charming, humorous. He was never grumpy or sulky and always woke to each new day with a quip that made me laugh. He saw the planet's happenings through wise and compassionate eyes. He was inspirational. He cared for his fellow man. For the time that he was in my life, there were so many moments where I felt in awe of how he saw the world. Few people can see the big picture and see a path that is the best for all. Grant could do that. I loved that about him.

He was also a romantic. Even after all those years together he would want to hold my hand every time we were out in public.

On car trips we would sing, harmonize, and look at each other with pleasure at remembering the words to the music of the 60s and 70s.

He would frequently and randomly pick a rose from our garden and give it to me. He was a man who spent ages at a card stand, choosing just the right one with the right words for my birthday, Christmas, or anniversary or just because. He was very loving and very charming.

But mankind is flawed. We're all flawed. No one is perfect.

Unfortunately, he looked outside of our marriage to meet a need. I cannot judge and say what that need was. Whether it was a sexual need or an ego-feeding need. Only Grant can answer that one.

But regardless, his pattern of seeking fresh grass belonged to him and was clear for anyone to see when viewing the trail of relationships in his past. Each long-term girlfriend and wife joined the pattern of the romantic side of his life. I bet each of us thought that he would be 'different this time', that 'we' have something 'unique', something 'very special' that he has not experienced to that depth before.

I reveal this about Grant really for context purposes. It's not my place to shine the spotlight on him except to give relevance to how the affair and subsequent separation and divorce affected my life and to include him in this to the extent that I have to show the back and forth of my narrative, as I reveal the battle that went on with my heart and my head.

In a broad sense, he was amazing… and for a very long time I loved him very much.

The bottom line though, is that although we both committed to be together, he must have felt okay with risking our relationship, betting that the strength of the glue that held he and I together would still hold us together through thick and thin. He used to tell me that he would never leave me.

But he risked us. He strayed outside of our agreement and finally fell in love with someone else. He and I were doomed.

And so, the story moves away from him and me and more into the steps I took to rebuild my life.

**A LEARNING MOMENT**

***THE OTHER GRASS IS ALWAYS GREENER***

The grass on the other side always appears to be greener, but ultimately, we find out that it is still just grass.

So, what's going to happen to our home grass without water? Well, it withers and ultimately dies.

What happens to the new grass getting watered? That grass grows and shines.

The areas where we put our attention, our energy, our affection, our love, is the grass we choose to water.

Think of a new relationship... right in the middle of that glorious first bloom. Oh, what heady days!

We take care of our appearance. We are considerate of our new partner's wants and needs. We aim to please. We talk kindly. We gently touch our partner. We want to spend time with them. We do things that we know will please them.

We water the grass... and what happens with all of that love energy? Oh, that grass flourishes.

Nature gears it that we love babies. Love kittens. Love puppies. They are all warm and snuggly and wonderful. We are drawn to them and want to hug and kiss and take care of them.

Nature gears it that we love new relationships. They get all of our attention. Usually, the other person sends the same energy back to us and there is blooming and flourishing and the world is wonderful.

Beautifully watered grass.

In some relationships, life gets in the way and the talk is of rent payments, activities that don't match, conflict about child raising. Dislikes rise to the surface, which put us right at the T-junction of choice again. We can become intolerant of our partner lying on the couch watching sport. Or we can choose to let them be who they are, doing what they love to do.

Sometimes, we can 'fall in love' and flow all of our energy into this new person and new relationship but somehow end up treating our friends with more respect than we show our partners.

## Chapter Twenty-Nine

# Am I Responsible?

Time went by, and I was still unable to fully accept that he had left me. That he had left 'us'.

How could he do that?

How could *she* push for a relationship with him when she knew about me? She knew he was married. Actually, she was married, too.

How could they do this to me?

And then, it struck me. This is a karmic universe and the realization of this hit me like bricks.

I had done a similar thing. Not to the extent of Grant's, but I had left my first husband and saw Grant as a better option. And now Grant was leaving me for Rachel. Around the time my first marriage was deteriorating, I saw that being with Grant was going to feed the needs that I thought were not being met. For me, Grant was greener grass.

***

I knew the words that Grant must have been saying to Rachel and how he was showering her with all of him.

She was being love-bombed.

He would have assured her that his and my marriage was over; he was probably saying it had been over for a long time.

But he hadn't told me that. And he hadn't acted that way with me.

I had to take a long hard look at myself.

I had to admit that what she was doing to me, I had done in my past.

It was time to dust off the mirror and see who I really was.

Was I the poor victim? No, I was reaping what I had sown. I was now experiencing what I had once made others experience. The time for being a victim was past. It was time I faced some real truth. I considered the people I had hurt most in my life and sat down and wrote out personal apology letters to each. The moment they were sent, I was done. I did not need any response or reply or discussion.

That was the precise moment that I took some responsibility for what I had done in my life and perhaps I was reaping a heavier version of what I had sown in my past? It was then that I knew the path that I had to take to be able to rebuild.

One such incident was when I was in my early twenties. I had always liked a guy in the wider circle of my friends and I had always hoped that he would ask me out. Around that time I was a travel consultant and on a consultant's trip to Australia one member of that group was rather nice and we sort-of clicked and it felt like we liked each other. Nothing happened. It was casual. Returning to New Zealand he said that although he lived in another city, one weekend he would come and see me. Sure. I was fine with that. So months later I hear from him and he is coming to see me. He would come to my home around seven and we can go out. This was okay. I looked forward to seeing him. However, that very afternoon I get a phone call from the local guy I really liked. He said that he would like to take me out. Wow. Heart pump. He went on to say he would like to take me out *that night*. Oh, what to do.

What I did was atrocious. I left a note for my travel consultant friend who had travelled all that way to see me. I left a note saying that I was sorry but something had come up and I couldn't meet him that night. I felt slightly sick. But I did it. What a disgusting thing to do. I never heard from him again.

He was one of the people I now apologized to.

The time for being a victim was over. I was entering the world of 'taking responsibility for my part in this current chaos and it felt right to have written those messages. To have started to clean up my own world. It not only felt right, it was right.

Grant didn't factor into this. He was just repeating the pattern of existence that was his entire love-life history. Woman. Affair. Leave. Repeat.

I was not his *be-all*, I was not the love of his life as he had professed. I was simply part of his repetitive cycle.

But while I took responsibility for having caused pain to others in the past, I wasn't ready to look at forgiving Grant… not yet.

I realized that in the bigger scheme of things, I was not really a total victim. I merely played my part in a repetitive cycle, and I needed to have a serious look at my own world to see my own cycles.

I was pleased that I had written to those that I had hurt, but digging deeper I also made the conscious decision to not be involved with any form of relationship ever again where another party was still present and involved and was possibly going to get hurt.

I didn't like that the fact that I had felt cavalier about another's feelings in the past. I had bought the line that the earlier relationship was over, without closely looking at anyone else to see if that was the truth.

I now wanted to live in truth.

Rose-colored glasses seem to have shields on their frames so that our vision is only on what is right in front of us and not the periphery.

If I had taken those glasses off and looked at the surroundings, I may have made other decisions. But that's the pull of love… It's so addictive…

It's incredibly hard to refuse that magnetic drug of attraction.

"Healing also means taking a look at the role you played in your own pain and suffering."

UNKNOWN

"You will never understand the damage you did to someone, until the same thing is done to you. That's why I am here."

KARMA

"The degree to which a person can grow, is directly proportional to the amount of truth they can accept about themselves without running away."

LELAND VAL DE WALL

## Chapter Thirty

## Unshackling The Chains

There came the moment when I realized that I was taking the hurt and anger forward into every new day. Carrying this load with us not only clouds our perception of each new day but when we are 'stuck' in the hurt, it does not seem possible to start to 'let go' and 'move on'.

I am not saying that we need to quickly forgive the very moment we are badly wounded and not be affected by the betrayal. That is unrealistic. Of course, we are affected. A bomb of destruction has gone off in our world and caused massive damage. But to get to the other side of the pain, grief and loss, we have to go through it.

To go through means facing reality. There comes a time where we need to turn and confront the reality of the situation head on, in order to start the process of unshackling the chains.

"Getting through" can occur by placing one foot in front of the other to slowly reach a point where we can confront the whole truth—and reality—of what has happened.

Coming to terms with the reality of the situation can sometimes be quite a process. For me, it was a lengthy process—a series of events, comments, and observations that slowly made me see what the truth was.

I am sure that these facts were there to be observed right at the beginning, but I was not ready to see them.

One such event was a Bonnie Raitt concert. I attended a twilight concert with some great friends on a beautiful vineyard lawn (at Matakana of all places) and sat about thirty feet from the woman herself on that warm summer night.

As the evening drew to an end, Bonnie picked up her guitar, sat on a stool, and started singing, *"I can't make you love me if you don't... You can't make the heart feel, something it won't..."*

Those words hit me. I couldn't make Grant's heart feel something it won't.

This moment was huge for me and was another step toward acceptance. The moment made me realize that our marriage was in his past and needed to be part of my past, too.

During the transition phase, when he was unsure about Rachel, he told me it would be easier to stay with me and not rock the boat, than to leave. But he was hoping for old feelings to surface again. He was hoping for the feelings he had about us to kick back in—to feel again the way he had felt about me once. He said that staying with me would be so much easier than the massive disruption his leaving would cause.

I see now that for him, the glow of the new love was too bright. Too shiny. Too new.

I had to come to terms with the reason he was choosing to be with her rather than with me.

I was battling this with logic, but the battle was not one that could be fought with logic. He was with her not because of how she looked, or her capabilities.

He was with her because of the way she made him *feel*.

...and there it was.

# Chapter Thirty-One

# Starting To Let Go

The realization that my battle was with emotion and not logic was a huge turning point. I remember what it was like to be in love. To be so besotted that any argument as to why I should not be with that person fell on deaf ears. Deep down I may have known a portion of any negative comments about the person to be true, but I had dived right in there, boots-and-all, 'feeling the feels.'

And there he was. Grant was right bang in the middle of feeling those feelings—and his rose-colored glasses were not looking at me.

I knew at that point that I had to retreat and care just for me. I had to stop wishing and hoping and I had to start genuinely trying to build an alternative life. A life without Grant.

Looking back, I find it fascinating that there was even the thought in my mind that I could possibly want to hang on to that marriage. He had gone. What was I trying to do? In hindsight, I can see that I was the little pig trying to rebuild my house with straw. Grant had blown up the strong foundations of 'us' and nothing was going to build that house again.

For years after the destruction, sometimes my heart ached. But I came to realize it did not ache for the man. It was illogical to want someone who hurt me on so many fronts. I didn't want the man anymore; I wanted all that we had built in our relationship. I did not necessarily want the physical things; I wanted the bonding things. I wanted to hang on to the closeness that comes from shared history. I wanted to stay wrapped in the cloth that was our marriage. Cloth that had been woven from the weft and warp of thousands of strands of moments.

So why did I dream about the feeling of slow dancing with him sometimes … sharing looks…having him tell me he loved me? Funny, I never dreamt about the pain of him being with someone else. My dreams were always about the good stuff.

The heart and the head surely resided in two different places.

# Chapter Thirty-Two

# Picking Up That First Brick In The Rebuild

There's a huge difference between a *healed* heart and a *closed* heart, and my work on myself was always geared towards healing. Even though my heart had been wounded, I did not want to live a life with a closed heart. Vulnerability means susceptibility to pain and loss. Vulnerability means putting our protection to the side and being open to experience. Yes, our hearts can be rocked about and even torn apart for a while. However, being in the arena where we are not sure, where we don't feel comfort, where we take the chance of saying 'I love you' first, where we find courage to have the experience—is *living*.

When someone closes their heart because they don't want to feel pain through possible loss; yes, they will most probably never experience all the hurtful emotions of loss. But they won't experience the joy of uninhibited love either.

They're not living a life—they're flat lining through existence.

We hear it when a person says that they won't ever let themselves love again. Their romantic experience left them scarred for life. How sad. That's like falling over on a hike and saying they'll never walk anywhere again. Yes, going through life without finding joy in our friends or lovers is a choice, but it comes with a very narrow band of feeling.

Even though my life had blown apart with Grant's decisions, it was still my life. It was up to me to take stock of the pieces that remained and it was also up to me, and no one else, to take those bits and shape them into the life that I wanted. A life that was possible and within my reach.

We own our story. We create our next chapters. If we don't consciously make each tiny decision that gears us toward the life we want, then life turns up any which way and we are but a spectator living what has been dealt to us.

When you are knocked out and flat on the ground, the only way is up.

Standing up and building a life takes courage and strength and by using the step-by-step mentality as well as the one-day-at-a-time expectation, we can get there. We get to feel better.

Every single day we wake up and face a simple decision first thing in the morning. It's the choice between "oh no" and pulling the sheets over our head, or saying "hello world" every morning. Saying the latter will mean that one day we wake and say "Hello World!" and mean it. We will feel it. Hello new day! It takes practice.

Initially, my teeth were clenched as I murmured a practiced 'hello' to the world. But, over time, I did experience that first day of a real feeling of joy as I said hello to the new day.

# Chapter Thirty-Three

# I Might Make It!

There came the time when I realized that I had survived it. I was alive and had a life. Not the life I had expected or thought I wanted, but it definitely was a life.

When I reached that point, it felt natural to look at the people who had betrayed me and consider how to genuinely let go. I no longer wanted to drag the chains of that life changing event into my future.

I reached that moment when I finally asked myself if I wanted to win him back. I realized that even if I did somehow get him back, having him in my life would not make me happy—not genuinely happy. There had been too many areas of destruction. While I had taken a certain amount of responsibility, the way he aborted the marriage right when we were in transition was incredibly cruel. He most probably felt that this was a good time as we had not yet signed a contract for our piece of land at Matakana or contracted a designer for our new home. But the bottom line was that Grant knew that I was at my most vulnerable—no job, no home, and no marriage. And he left.

I had a dream one night. I see now how metaphoric it was.

In my dream, Grant was on a boat—a nice ski-boat; the type you enjoy on a lake. There was a rope tied to a rubber dingy coming off the back of the boat. I was in that dingy. Grant had stopped driving the big boat and we were both bobbing in the water in our separate craft. He reached down to me with what I thought was an open hand. I reached my hand up to be pulled on board and watched him cut the rope between us. Instead of pulling me onto our bigger boat, he left me in the dingy. Instead of the two of us continually creating the next steps of our married life, he cut me adrift.

I was left in my dingy bobbing in water watching him slowly power away from me.

When I look at that metaphor, I see that that is exactly what happened. He was gone. He had left me to bob in that water alone.

Standing up again from all of that loss was not easy. But the idea that all I had to do was to place one foot in front of the other worked for me. All I had to do in my mind was get through one day at a time.

'Letting go' did not mean I had to condone his actions or accept the perceived injustice heaped upon me. Forgiveness did not mean that I approved of Grant's actions.

I recognized that loss and sadness should have their timeframe within me. They too need to be lived through. However, I had to make a decision about that catastrophic event and determine how I would accommodate it in my life.

Was it going to be the thing that defined me?

Was it going to be something that poisoned me from enjoying new, fulfilling relationships?

A friend who was devastated by betrayal said to me that he will never fall in love again, or trust someone, for fear of getting hurt.

When I heard him say that, I knew it was not the case for me.

Yes, my heart had been broken. And, yes, the pain of that was intolerable.

But I love loving someone. And I love having someone love me.

A lot of us have baggage from past relationships, but I wanted to properly, fully, and completely deal with this baggage to the best of my ability, so that I only took 'carry-on luggage' forward into my new life.

Again, I encountered a T-junction... A new choice of going right or left.

The choice in front of us could be that we are going to continue to allow this 'event' to define who we are. Or we can take a look at our life as a whole and see this incident as a drop in the graph, a low point, but not the total of who we are or the life we have had or the life we have yet to experience. It was a 'part' of our existence.

"You either get bitter or you get better. It's that simple. You either take what has been dealt to you allowing it to make you a better person, or you allow it to tear you down. The choice does not belong to fate, it belongs to you."

JACK SHIPP

"You can't really begin to appreciate life until it has knocked you down a few times. You can't really begin to appreciate love until your heart has been broken. And you can't really begin to appreciate happiness until you've known sadness. Once you've walked through the valley, the view from the mountain top is breath-taking."

SUSAN GALE

> "Given a choice between grief and nothing, I'd choose grief."
>
> — WILLIAM FAULKNER

*Gaynor Morrissey*

"That shit may have broken your heart but it opened your eyes.
Take the win."

THEPROMISESKEPT

# Chapter Thirty-Four

# Is It Possible To Be Truly Happy Again?

How do you move from the pain and the loss and the betrayal to somewhere better?

For me, this is where the concept of gratitude came into the picture.

We've all heard about the benefits of practicing gratitude. I have been somewhat cynical about platitudes and new-age statements, such as practice gratitude. But this time, I made a decision to give the concept of gratefulness a go.

For me, it started when I noticed a flower. One little flower.

I was consciously taking note of the flower, the texture, and the complexity of the bloom, and the way the light lit it. And I thought it was so amazingly beautiful.

That was the moment where the build-back really started for me. That one little flower.

I decided at that moment that every day, I would note at least one thing that I appreciated. It might time spent with a friend, or a photo that looks great or something that smells wonderful.

I would consciously note that I saw beauty in it, or felt appreciation for the phone call, or breathed some conscious breaths while looking at the sky.

I made it an exercise. A forced happening. Something that I had to do every day, like physical exercise.

I did this consciously and found, over time, that it became an unconscious habit. Slowly, my world started to fill with things that gave me warmth, joy, and happiness.

The balance of my world, which had been heavily weighted in grief, started to shift. I had fewer moments of sadness and more of happiness. It didn't happen overnight, but feeling better and eventually feeling good began to gather speed.

My world was filled with whatever I put my attention to. When I was buried in grief, I was buried in the grief. When I poked my head above the sadness and started to see things that were warm and good and beautiful, good things started to manifest in my world. Some areas were even great.

The more I focused on the good and great and the warm, the more my world filled with these senses. Our worlds are what we see. Our world fills with that which we put our attention on. We know this to be true. When a loved one passes on, our world is filled with sadness and grief. When something great has happened like a new birth in the family, our world is filled with joy.

"Perception is a key component to gratitude. And gratitude a key component to joy."

AMY WEATHERLEY

## A LEARNING MOMENT

### *THIS IS MAGIC!*

We radiate what we feel and the big secret is that we can change how we feel inside simply by making the decision and living it. I know this can sound 'new-age mumbo-jumbo'... but it works. Give it a go.

Time passed, and I moved from my central apartment to a tiny home in the outskirts of Auckland City. I loved it. This cottage was surrounded by bush, and I felt very safe and comfortable. It felt very 'me'. While my new home surroundings were great, the move meant that I had a greater distance to travel to work. I took the train some days. It was easier than sitting in my car stuck in traffic. On those train days, I could listen to music or simply sit and look out the window.

One day while on the train heading to work, I felt very sad. It was the middle of winter. I had to get up really early to catch the train to get to the city to sit at my desk and do a job. This was not how I envisaged my life being at that age. Things looked bleak. I felt low.

Suddenly, the words my mother used to say to me popped into mind. "If you want to be happy, then *be* happy. If you want a friend, *then be a friend*." I decided that when I got off the train and walked the distance to work, I would make eye contact with everyone I saw and give them a small smile. Almost everyone smiled back. By the time I arrived at work I felt good. I walked in the door with a cheery "Well, hi there everyone"!"

A simple technique but a good one. A practical one, and one that provides instant results.

"If you inherently long for something, become it first.
If you want gardens, become the gardener.
If you want love, embody love.
If you want mental stimulation, change the conversation.
If you want peace, exude calmness.
If you want to fill your world with artists, begin to paint.
If you want to be valued, respect your own time.
If you want to live ecstatically, find the ecstasy within yourself.
This is how to draw it in, day by day, inch by inch."

VICTORIA ERICKSON

"Smiling is infectious, you catch it like the flu, when someone smiled at me today, I started smiling too.
I passed around the corner and someone saw my grin. When he smiled, I realized, I'd passed it on to him.
I thought about that smile, then I realized its worth. A single smile, just like mine could travel round the earth. So, if you feel a smile begin, don't leave it undetected. Let's start an epidemic quick, and get the world infected"!

SPIKE MILLIGAN

# Chapter Thirty-Five

# Do I Have To Forgive?

I was still trying to fully accept the concept of 'forgiveness'.

I had reached a stage where I made the conscious decision to look at everything I appreciated about Grant. All of the things that having him in my life for so many years gave to me.

It took some time, but I came to feel good about the experience of us having been together, rather than sad that he was no longer in my life.

While Grant had been a huge piece of my life, the end of us was no longer the focus of my life. He was a *part* of my life. Some great chapters were written because we had some amazing times over many years.

The feeling of loss about those memories slowly changed to appreciation that I had had them. I started to laugh with friends about some of the fun things Grant and I had done, as well as some of his unusual idiosyncrasies, his little mannerisms and habits.

I could mention his name and not cry.

I could think about something that had happened between us and not feel loss. I began to feel okay that we had once been an 'us'.

I started to not think about him for days, sometimes quite a few days at a time. Then he would pop into my mind in random flashes and when that happened, I mainly felt okay.

For some time, even when I was feeling better about things overall, I would experience pangs of loss. But they became moments, no longer a place where I lived.

I came to realize that loss is not something you 'get over' and return to how you were. If we're lucky, the experience can move us into a greater space. One which has a huge appreciation for life.

I no longer experienced daily grief. No aching longing. The major upset in my life had changed and become a sort of appreciation for what Grant and I had shared in our time together.

I don't know that I will ever truly feel fine about the shattering of my world. But the nuclear bomb and destruction no longer defined who I was. It was a horrible experience, but it was not who I am.

I had come through.

There comes a time where we have to face the reality of what happened to us. If we want to be in the present and not stuck in the past, then we need to look at that tiger, head on.

I had faced the horror and survived. I faced the truth and somehow found a taproot of strength that pulled me through.

*What doesn't kill you, makes you stronger.* It's a cliché, but there is an element of truth in the overused expression.

In the early days, weeks, and sometimes years, there are moments we fear we may not survive.

But we can survive.

Grieving takes as long as it takes.

Sometimes, we think this emotional explosion has destroyed who we are and who we were, and we will never be more than a shell of who we once were.

Avoidance could seem like the easiest path; we try to distract ourselves from the internal pain. Many people turn to drink, food, or drugs, craving the distraction so they can feel okay, even for a small unit of time. Sometimes the feeling is overwhelming and we just want it to end.

For some, ending the pain means jumping straight into a new relationship, carrying their toxic baggage across to the new stage. I have never seen success come out of this strategy.

While they might feel the rush of the fresh good times, it doesn't last. Actually, it can't last.

Unless we are in a relatively healed space, then replacement seldom equals long-term happiness.

The only way to fully deal with something is to face it, fully and completely. If there is pain from a loss, one needs to work at recovery; to sit with the loss and view it straight on. This is hard. And it takes time.

I faced my hell without avoidance (apart from the shopping!), but I am the first to admit that if I had stopped crying long enough in those early days to notice that someone else wanted me, I may well have jumped into those arms.

Trying to feel good is not a mistake. But rapidly entering new relationships, turning to drink, and taking drugs are all efforts to feel better and are elements of avoidance; they don't actually work in the long run.

If we find ourselves in a rabbit-hole, a huge step toward getting out is simply recognizing that the 'solution' we are thinking of grabbing most probably might not be the best thing for us in the long run.

If we are to recover, really recover, then sooner or later we need to rip the Band-Aid off and let that wound genuinely heal. At some stage, we need to face what happened and our part in in, without crutches or feel-good alternatives.

I ended up making it through every agonizing day. It took some time, but for me, it was the best way to handle it. Improvement was slow. It felt like how, during the change of seasons, each day brings one or two more minutes of day-light as we head into spring and summer. It is not an instant thing. It is a slow process but summer comes. One day at a time.

"There are two ways to be happy: change the situation, or change your mindset towards it."

ALEN G

"Look back and be grateful. Look ahead and be hopeful."

ANONYMOUS

"We can let the circumstances of our lives harden us so that we become increasingly resentful and afraid, or we can let them soften us and make us kinder. You always have the choice."

DALAI LAMA

> "When you want different for yourself you have to start moving differently. Old keys don't unlock new doors."
>
> — ALEXANDRU GALOS

# Chapter Thirty-Six

# Some Help Along The Way

I have a close buddy who lost her husband through cancer. They had been a couple for most of her adult life and she was well into her seventies when I met her. She was one of the few people that I had shared my breakup and aftermath with, and when I told her that if I saw a quote or phrase on Instagram or social media that resonated with me in a positive way, I would take a photo of it and keep it as part of a collection in a folder in my phone. I found these motivational and uplifting. She responded that when her husband had passed, she saved every photo she could find of someone smiling.

We had developed a similar coping mechanism.

Those photos of people smiling kept reminding her that life goes on and people can be happy. My quotes gave me the same comfort. There are universal truths and when we are reminded of a truth, it resonates within us and often aids the way we view things.

***

Sometimes facing even the good memories is hard; when that memory, once treasured, now comes with a sting.

It took a long time before I could look at photos of Grant and me and not feel a pang. But not long ago, I watched our wonderful wedding video and loved it—although I fast-forwarded over the vows. Even though I haven't healed 100%—as I couldn't not watch our faces promising our vows—I'd come a long way and I've now reached a place of peace.

We may never fully recover, but that's okay. Our experiences—good and bad—make us who we are. We all have scars. The question is, do we let them ruin the rest of our life? Or do we somehow move on?

I watched that wedding video feeling appreciative of the fantastic occasion, seeing friends and family celebrating, and I felt okay.

*Gaynor Morrissey*

"The best feeling ever is realizing you're not sad anymore over something you thought you would never get over."

UNKNOWN

## Chapter Thirty-Seven

# Some Relationships Are Just Crap

Getting past our pain is not always rainbows and happy endings. There are some circumstances where the situation was so awful that there is no real way to feel good about that relationship, ever. It was just too toxic.

In those situations, it's probably best to put the full-stop at the end of it and leave it all in our past.

Once we have recovered sufficiently to take a peek back at the relationship, though, it's still helpful and healthy, to look at any area where we could possibly take some responsibility for our part. And there usually is some part where we need to be truthful with ourselves.

While there are scenarios where the weight of responsibility and wrong-doing is clearly heavier on one side, in most marriage breakups, both partners contributed to the failure of the relationship—no matter how big and small the fault.

Think it over. Admit any fault or wrongdoing, even if it is just to yourself. And then let that stuff go.

## A LEARNING MOMENT

### *DIFFERENT ENDINGS*

Not all marriages or relationships can have a happy ending. With breakups and divorces there are sometimes others to consider, such as children.

When children are involved, it can be challenging to not dump our disappointment, fury, and resentment all over them. We have to consciously separate our relationship with our partner from our children's relationship with their parent.

A good friend used to phone me and verbally dump all over her husband to me while they were going through a rough breakup. Her children were small, and they were often present. At times they'd be in the back of the car while she ranted over the phone.

I'd ask, "Is it a good idea that the children hear this?" She would generally respond with; "They know what he's like," or "They'll be okay. They have to face the realities of life."

Her children are now in their mid-twenties, and they are struggling with their own relationships. They can only be with their mother or father on separate occasions. They live a life where they are constantly conscious that what they say to one parent, they can't say to the other. That's quite a load to lay on our kids.

# Chapter Thirty-Eight

# Reflections: What Can We Do Differently?

When my world finally settled—or at least began to settle—I looked back at the areas in my marriage that I could have experienced differently. Areas when I might have looked at situations from a different point of view, or a little more deeply.

No one is perfect. There were moments where I wasn't the best partner, or I did not behave the way I should have. That is part of relationships.

I wish I had realized earlier that communication styles differ between men and women. Men and women are Mars and Venus.

Men are more likely to want to get straight to the nub of the problem and find a solution. Women generally like to debrief, fully detailing the bits and pieces of the scenario. Though this is a generalization, it applies to lots of situations.

I would have loved to have a good template of communication, to learn to ask, "Do you want me to just listen to what you have to say and support you? Or do you want me to hear the story and suggest a solution?"

Do you want a listener, or do you need a solution? It's a simple concept but a huge one—to ask for what you need, but also to ask what your partner needs on this day, in this situation.

To feel heard is powerful. Communication is just not talking. A real skill is being present and able to truly hear what is being said to us.

Too often we say, "No... no... just listen to me, I am trying to tell you something." But people are not mind readers. It's over to us to say "Hey, I just need to vent about something, and I need you to please just listen right now."

I wish I had known about this earlier and applied it more often, not just with my own needs but with my interactions with others. Simply being there for someone, listening to their words and not having to jump in with guidance and advice is a powerful communication tool and can be a great comfort for others.

I have been surprised learning about the power of viewpoints. Our own viewpoint is our story we wrap around scenarios. Two people who are close can experience a single event considerably differently. An example of this could be a husband and wife are out to dinner with a couple, she might be a long-term female friend and on this night, they meet her new husband. The two husbands chat about sport and seem to get on well. On the way home, the wife is quiet. She thinks about how disappointed she is that this was a rare evening where she and her husband could enjoy a night out without the kids and he hardly gave her any attention. He, on the other hand, feels okay that he liked the other guy and found some common ground with him and he's sure his wife would be proud of him for making the effort with the new male. They both drive home in silence. Him feeling good; her feeling resentful. One evening out results in two separate viewpoints. Two separate outcomes.

Communication is the glue that keeps all good relationships intact. Being able to express how we feel and to be understood is magic dust. On the other hand, to just listen to the other person and be open to hearing their viewpoint without waiting for them to finish so they can listen to us, is such a gift to the relationship. I wish I had known about this earlier. Oh, I'd known about it. But I didn't apply it.

A huge realization for me is that while I think I am a reasonably good communicator and I know that Grant certainly is, there were areas of our relationship we did not speak about. I now know that I didn't fully communicate my wants and needs in the marriage and so how did I expect Grant to have made an effort to meet my needs? I think I automatically expected him to know. In hindsight, that was not fair of me.

## Chapter Thirty-Nine

## Being Right. Look Out, This One's A Real Kicker

In order to be *right* about something – to justify being right, the other person in the scenario needs to be made *wrong*.

When we do something against our partner, we justify our actions by convincing ourselves that we are right and they are wrong.

This applies to most areas of life. The person who cheats on an expense claim from his employer can justify it by thinking 'Well, they have heaps of money anyway and besides, they haven't given me a pay rise in years…I am not getting paid enough.'

The man who cheats on his partner justifies his action by starting to view his partner differently. 'She's more interested in her work friends than me. I'm not even sure that she still loves me!'

Not only is one partner cheating, but they're making the other person wrong. First in their own thoughts and then by their actions.

The one who is being cheated on is also being criticized for little things, with no idea of why.

Now there are arguments, and the beginning of the breakdown of the relationship.

This concept of making the other person 'wrong' to justify being 'right' is cruel. It's another slap for the victim. Not only are they getting hit due to the acts secretly being committed against them, but they are also the target of the justifications so that the perpetrator can be right in their own heads.

The husband whose wife is flirting with the neighbor gets trounced when she criticizes her husband to her friends. 'He's such a lazy sod! He would rather spend all the weekend doing other stuff than giving me attention.'

When this happens, the communication between the couple is no longer clean, nor is it honest. The partner who is making the other wrong to make themselves right usually ends up viewing their partner through new lenses. They see faults, flaws that justify why they are so 'right' for doing the harmful action, such as having an affair.

There cannot be an affair that has no consequences for the marriage. It's impossible.

The one having the affair might have gotten away with the rendezvous without being caught in the act, but they know deep inside that these actions are harmful to the marriage. Their home is burning. They are just not fully aware of it.

There must have been times where Grant came home to me after being with Julie, when he would not have wanted to sit down for a nice chat about our individual days. I am sure that while I was 'home' for him, that he must have felt a level of discomfort at those times. I would like to think there was. I would like to think that he had some form of guilt

If you are taking actions that are harmful, there is always a consequence. If you are not doing the things you should be doing, that's also harmful.

*** 

An outside person cannot break up a happy and tight marriage.

When I look back with clear eyes, I can see that Grant had been telling me about areas where he wasn't the happiest. Also, he had mentioned a few times that men seem to become redundant when grandchildren come along.

Perhaps his perception that he was no longer as important was because he was aging. Grandchildren often coincide with a time when men are not as physically strong. Their sons are fitter and stronger than they are. Sometimes the workplace has new younger talent with fresh ideas.

"Before you get sick; your body will whisper about its fatigue. Before you break up, your lover will whisper their requests. Before your business goes bankrupt, your customers will whisper their complaints. If you don't listen to the whispers, you'll be forced to hear the screams."

AUBREY MARCUS

*Gaynor Morrissey*

\*\*\*

Many marriages are now breaking apart after twenty, thirty, and even forty years together. We should look at this and question why it's happening.

One big change has been that little blue pill, helping men to maintain their sexuality longer. But it's not always the men who want a different life. Some women really suffer with menopause, which can affect her sex drive.

Maybe because we are all living longer, the concept of staying with the same person forever no longer applies. In a human sense, we have done our duty and procreated, and the offspring are surviving by themselves in the great wide world, so the man and woman who have raised a family look at each other and review their decision about staying together. One partner might want to move to the country and fish. The other wants to stay in the city, in the home in which they built their life.

I am not saying that staying together is right. Conversely, I am not promoting breakups. I am merely observing that so many marriages seem to be ending later in life than ever before in history. My comment about Viagra applies here. Maybe some men have a new lease on life (so to speak) and feel the charge and youthfulness again and see a whole sea of bountiful fish out there and feel it's time to return to their youth (not that they can) and play the field again. Who knows?

An acquaintance of mine, Loren, was married. Both husband and wife were in second marriages. They were together for many years. When they were in their later life (she in her sixties and he, early seventies), he left her. She was devastated. Learning about this, I also discovered that her parents were unwell and that she has grandchildren on her side of the family. Apparently, her focus had been caring for her ailing parents and enjoying the grandchildren. And the husband? He wanted to travel, and while I am sure he loved his wife, he had looked at the movie of how the rest of his life was going to play out and he left her. I do see some parallels with my own scene albeit not really the same as Grant and I were about to start a great new chapter together in Matakana.

Loren remains in the same home that they shared and is trying to carry on with her life, but she is reportedly constantly in anger and grief and of the view that his leaving means that the rest of her life looks rather bleak. The first bit of advice I would give her would be to move from that home and start afresh by herself. Some folks sit in the same lounge they shared with their partners looking at the rocker that hubby sat in for a million nights. That would be living torture. Staying in the same environment can keep a person 'stuck' in a moment. Every day their environment screams 'loss'.

**A LEARNING MOMENT**

***CHANGE IS POSSIBLE***

When there is a loss of a partner or spouse due to the relationship ending, the question can arise as to what to do with the living arrangements.

My advice would be that when you are ready, if you can, move to a different home. Stop being constantly reminded of loss by staying in the environment you shared with your partner. Move somewhere else. Get furniture that you want. Make it fresh. Buy or create the art that you want. Make a garden that you like the shape of. Paint the internal walls of your home in colors that you like. Join groups that you want to. Best to stay within your budget, though!

There is time for sitting in the loss and there is a time to end that and create something different.

We are the only ones who can decide which is best for us.

Recovery has to start with the basics.

Get plenty of rest. Eat food that is good for you. Stay active. Find as much physical comfort as you can. Get a massage, go for a walk, or lounge on the couch and watch a movie. Treat yourself with whatever gives you some comfort —in moderation.

Find a trusted confidant. Expressing your feelings to another person aids the healing process.

These action steps are what we can focus on doing.

Often when we find ourselves in despair, we ask, "What can I do? I don't know what to do!"

Initially, we don't need to do anything. If we are experiencing a devastating event, it's best to not do anything for a little while. To cope with loss, we have to first absorb the reality of the situation. And that is not always something that we can do quickly.

To begin with, just stop. Give yourself time to absorb the shock.

This sometimes happens naturally as our bodies go into a slow-motion phase of disbelief.

## A LEARNING MOMENT

### *AVOIDING THE RABBIT HOLE*

It's incredibly easy when experiencing shock and loss to lose ourselves in the process. Avoiding this takes supreme effort, and it comes at the very time when there is depleted energy, low self-esteem, and a complete loss of enthusiasm.

There is a right time to sit with the pain and the shock, but there is also the right time to take a first step to avoid sliding down the slippery slope of hopelessness.

Ironically, that self-imposed routine in Canada when I was getting out of bed, walking, eating good food, doing my make-up... Each of those small efforts contributed greatly to the rebuilding of my self-esteem.

Here are some simple recovery steps:

Get out of bed every day.

Make that bed.

Shower.

Eat.

Step outside and look at the sky, or study a flower

Visit a beautiful place, a park, a beach or an art gallery.

Go for a short walk.

Compliment one person with something positive you have noticed about them. "Hey, I just had to say, that scarf looks amazing on you." Don't wait for the response... just walk away.

Notice something good about the environment. Is it the heat of the sun on your face? The smell of the air? The color of a plant?

Consciously breathe. In through the nose... hold for the count of four... and then slowly release out through the mouth. Better still, press your tongue to the roof of your mouth and feel more oxygen enter your lungs.

Plan a meal. Take your time preparing that meal and slowly eat the food.

Take a nap if you need to. Only a nap; don't stay in bed.

"One way to calm an anxious mind is to notice when you are doing okay. It may be fleeting.
The concept of 'being okay' may only be there for a short space of time. But make sure you notice that for that timeframe, you were doing okay."

RICK HANSON

**A LEARNING MOMENT**

*SOME HELPFUL STEPS TO FEELING BETTER*

When I look back on the trek from the nuclear explosion to personal contentment and everything along the way, I think that if I were to give advice to someone, I would break down my guide into some steps that could be summarized as:

Find someone—anyone—who you can blubber to. Talking it out helps to get it out and talking puts words around feelings. Understanding where the feelings come from makes it easier to find answers to your predicament.

Embrace any comforts you can find: soothing baths, massages, or anything that leaves you feeling better.

Take the time you need to wallow. Coming to terms with devastating loss does not have a timer. We move to our own timeline. But guard against becoming stuck in that place.

Avoid reacting or responding when you are emotionally distraught.

Find a good counsellor if you need one. Don't bottle things up.

When you are ready, face the tiger. But only when you are ready. To truly heal, one needs to face the reality.

Never make a major decision without taking some time and space to let it breathe or percolate in your mind.

*\*\*\**

There is a secret to starting the process of feeling better.

This step comes a little way along the path of healing. Initially, we are so hurt or angry and the idea of feeling nice about the other person seems absurd. There will come a time though, when we realize that life is not going to be the same. That relationship has ended, and we start to look at what our future might be. Our world has been full of loss. Maybe it's time to fill it with something else.

The secret is to start the process of changing our perspective. Appreciating the fact that we had the experience, being grateful that we had those bonds. Grateful that we felt such love.

This can be our gift to ourselves.

If we allow hatred, anger, and regret, to define our lives, we are not doing ourselves any favors.

Feeling grateful for the one little flower started me on a path of filling my life with self-love, goodness, and appreciation for all that I now have. And physically it is not much, but I love every single thing in my life.

"The miracle of gratitude is that it shifts your perception to such an extent that it changes the world you see."

DR ROBERT HOLDEN

"Practicing gratitude can shift your focus on positive things which can increase your happiness.
Additionally, if you understand the Law of Attraction, you can't attract more of something if you are ungrateful for what you already have.
If you focus on being grateful for something, you are opening yourself up to receive more of what you are grateful for.
If you focus on what you don't have, then you are opening yourself to attracting the same old experience you've always had."

MIKE SYGULA

"In the blink of an eye, everything can change. So forgive often and love with all your heart. You may not have that chance again."

ZIG ZIGLAR

## Chapter Forty

# Is It Time To Stick My Toe In The Water...Again?

After about a year, my wonderful savior, Wendy, started suggesting the concept of dating again. Me? Go on a date? The idea seemed so foreign, but after many weeks of her gently prodding, I thought I would give it a go.

I registered with an online dating site and put up a profile, making it as real as I could—warts and all.

This strategy must have appealed to some really nice guys.

So, my profile was up and then I waited. I enjoyed immense pleasure from the flow of interest. It gave my tattered ego a real boost. Someone finds me interesting? These people want to meet me?

This was a new space for me and I wanted to go slow. After a while, I started to sort the wheat from the chaff.

When we are young, we are often attracted by physical looks. But now, I was more interested in their viewpoints on life. Their interests. But I also wanted chemistry if it was there. I found myself more interested in the profile narrative than their photos. I felt a flicker of attraction to those who wrote with humor and appeared to have more depth, rather than those saying they loved nature and walking on the beach at sunrise. (I came to think that I didn't need to be on a dating site. I just needed to go to the beach to see all these lonely, amazing people greeting each day.)

I made the decision that should I date, I was not going to talk about Grant, but rather just say that I had been married and it didn't work out. My experience was not going to be blurted out to every Tom, Dick, and Harry.

Braving a few coffees and dinners, I came to see that the sea has some sharks in it, some handsome strong fish who were rather empty headed, and some bigoted, biased peeps who were not very open-minded. Most of these dates revealed rare glimpses of like-minded souls.

Those that saw the world as I did were few indeed, and after a few weeks, I decided to close shop.

Just as that door was shutting, I received a call from a well-known city doctor who had recently split from his long-term partner. We chatted, and I was surprised to realize the first call lasted a couple of hours. This man took my interest. We arranged to meet. I felt a little excited.

Two days before that first date, he phoned. His long-term girlfriend had been around to see him, and they had decided to reconcile. That was a bit of a blow, but the previous couple of years had hit me a lot harder. This felt like a feather across the face. I was not upset, but I ended up spending that New Year's Eve alone.

On New Year's Day, I revisited some of the profiles of those who had reached out to me. I found a photo of a guy, sitting, holding a coffee cup. He was a photographer with his artworks behind him, wearing jeans with bare feet. I had never seen such beautiful hands. The way he held that mug and just looked at the camera, spoke to me.

I responded to his initial message and there started a friendship that has lasted. We think similarly regarding politics. Our viewpoints on the world align, and his humor is outstanding. He lives in the South Island of New Zealand, so meeting up immediately was not going to happen.

In fact, through the years, we have never met. We have never spoken on the phone. We have not seen each other in person, but we have had this amazing digital relationship. One I treasure. Something will happen on the planet and I will get a text and the debate will begin. He calls me his "EF"—his 'ethereal friend'. And just the other day his message told me how I was the light in his dark night. The one person he can tell anything to.

From those coffees and dinners, I found two people who I have remained the best of friends with to this day. One tells me that should he ever get married, I am his choice for best 'man' to stand for him.

Fulfilling companionship comes in many forms.

"I'm now actually extremely grateful that some things didn't work out the way I once wanted them to."

UNKNOWN

*Gaynor Morrissey*

"When you think
That the mountains too high;
That the sea is too wide …. and you'll never get through.
But some way…
Somehow…
Somehow, you do."

REBA MCENTIRE "SOMEHOW YOU DO"
FROM THE MOVIE FOUR GOOD DAYS

"It is when you are going through the most difficult chapter of life that your hero is revealed, and how beautiful when you finally realize... you have the strength to save yourself."

DODINSKY

# Chapter Forty-One

# In Our Lives For A Reason Or A Season

This chapter contains quotes from Tyler Perry as the alter ego Madea... I just love Tyler Perry and the video clip in which 'Madea' speaks to her son. It goes like this;

*If somebody wants to walk out of your life, Let. Them. Go. Especially if you know you have done everything you can. You've been the best man or woman you can be and they still want to go, let Them Go.*

*... Some come* (into your life) *for a lifetime. Some come for a season. You got to know which is which.*

Madea then puts people into the category of a tree (and I paraphrase below).

The 'leaves' blow every which way. They're not stable and can fly away with the wind. They're not really on your team.

The 'branches' can make you think they are a good friend but the moment you do 'something wrong' they step on you. They betray you. They are not good friends although they appeared to be initially.

Then there's the 'roots' of the tree. These are the few that are in your life for the good and the bad. They hold you up. They don't go away. These are real friends. And they don't keep score.

Madea goes on to say, *"Nobody said* (life) *will be easy, but it gets easier when you learn how to love yourself. You need to learn to be by yourself. People have to learn how to be alone. If you don't know how to be by yourself, what are you going to do with somebody else? Go work on you"*.

Sound advice, Madea. We are all better in a relationship, friendship, or a marriage when we are okay with who we are. The best relationships are when we contribute within them and we are the best partner or the best friend we can be. It comes from self-love and being comfortable with ourselves.

I'm now fussy. When I notice that a friend or colleague is continually draining my life energy, I gently move aside from them.

It's a good idea to take a personal check on who we have in our lives. If someone in our life makes us feel drained every time they've been in our space for a while, take another look at that relationship. I'm not talking about the friend who is upset because something upsetting has happened in their lives. That's a fleeting thing and we can feel good that they have turned to us for comfort. I'm talking about the ones who drain the marrow from our soul.

From time to time, most of us have had such people in our lives. They take our energy and leave us dry. I didn't know what was happening at the time, as I felt a sense of long-term loyalty to these people. But they were not good for me. They left me feeling flat.

My way of handling such situations was not a major break-up drama, but simply a gentle shift in my availability. Before long, they had moved on to someone else.

I feel it's best to surround ourselves with positive people when we can. Being positive will attract positivity.

A play on my mother's advice could be, "If you want a good and loyal friend, then be a good and loyal friend."

## A LEARNING MOMENT

### *FOOD FOR THOUGHT*

Here are some concepts and actions steps to help you view things in a more positive way. These are some of the things I tried—some consciously and others unconsciously.

Viewing things differently alters and changes our viewpoint.

Rather than holding on to the feeling of animosity or upset, try to find something you appreciate. Just one thing.

By changing our internal patterns, we change the reality around ourselves and therefore affect and influence everyone else around us.

It's how we behave within our world that changes realities.

Some have a fear of being on their own. Learn to live alone. Learn to like your own company.

I started to become conscious of where I was going to put all of my attention and energy. I knew that I had to shed being 'stuck' in that loss. I would ask myself 'Are my actions in this moment keeping me in the loss or are my actions and energy, my time, my beliefs, and my hope moving me toward feeling better?'

Our emotional charge runs through us all the time, fueled by our perceptions and thoughts. Emotional charge itself is not right or wrong, neither good nor bad. Emotional charge is the color of our lives. There's nothing wrong with it. The question is, where are we going to direct it?

Make compassionate choices.

Remember that how you react to every situation will speak of who you are.

Think of your everyday world as lines of possibility.

Make the conscious decision to feel okay about each and every day.

Move away from constricting habits in order to move into a new direction.

Be willing to open up to new ways of seeing things.

Every great change begins with a single decision.

It's fine to feel the grief of loss, but experience it for its time. Make the decision that this is not where we are going to live. That can be the first decision; 'this is not where I am going to live'. Say it out loud.

Say to yourself; *'Now, I choose to…* (and make the conscious choice). *'I choose to see things differently. I see my future positively'*.

Choose new ways of behaving.

Be responsible for your thoughts and energy. Where we put our thoughts and energies is where our lives will go. When we keep spinning in the pattern of despair, our lives will continue spinning there. Shift thoughts and energy to the possibility of hope and your life will start to turn in those directions.

"Remember, happiness doesn't depend upon who you are or what you have; It depends solely on what you think."

DALE CARNEGIE

## Chapter Forty-Two

## Karma And Forgiveness.
## Do They Go Hand-In-Hand?

Our western-world way of looking at karma falls along the lines of 'What you sow, so shall you reap.' 'What you give is what you get.' 'If you do something bad, be careful, because it will come back to you and knock you in the teeth.'

I have always held the belief that you reap what you sow, that somehow, we cop back what we have done. Sometimes, I have ignored that in my life but sooner or later, that whack has come along.

Recently, I have looked a little deeper into the concept of karma and how it relates to energy.

We all have our own emotional charge running through us all of the time. The question is; Where are we going to direct it?

Let's say we have an argument with somebody, so, for the next while, we can't stop thinking about it. How many people within the first little while of meeting them tell us all about the bad things that someone has done to them? That's a lot of entrapped energy. That person's focus, thoughts, conversations, emotional charge, is all caught in that incident. They have charge with the other person in that incident and it will keep calling them back until they have resolved it.

It's better to resolve it. It always is.

If we hold onto the unresolved conflict with a person and we refuse to forgive them, we actually go through our life energetically linked to that person.

We are the ones carrying that unresolved energy.

We can either go through our life living this to the end, or we can handle it by becoming consciously responsible for it. It's our choice. It's easier to be consciously responsible than to be unconsciously reliving the pattern until it is resolved.

Karma is not a punishment. It is unresolved emotional charge. And the pattern will repeat until it is resolved.

Whenever we don't take responsibility for our unresolved charge and don't bring it to resolution and healing, then the unresolved trauma often has a reaction. An example of this is the woman who dislikes that her partner is a big drinker. They fight all the time over this. It's a horrible situation. Then they break up and she rapidly moves on to another partner, and ironically, he is a serious drinker too. Why does this woman seem to attract partners who live this way?

Let's keep looking at 'energy' that is stuck and not resolved.

It seems that the universe is geared for us to repeat scenarios until they are handled. Patterns will re-emerge until they are cleared, handled, resolved.

This is not always obvious or conscious.

We can clear this energy through resolution. And part of that resolution is forgiveness.

Forgiving the one who has done us wrong seems unfair. They did harm to us, and we have to fix it?

No, we don't have to 'fix it'. We don't have to tidy up the injustice. But we can help *ourselves* by finding a way to clear the blocked energy that holds us to the sadness, the badness. It's for us and for our own future. It's how we move forward.

We make a choice as to how we are going to deal with this.

Being angry over an event, or over the way we're treated, is a natural emotion. But if we continue to be angry, we need to look at our own involvement in the situation. The secret is taking responsibility for our own charge. Our own part in it.

Energy is just like electricity. It has no consciousness. If we take responsibility for this energy, then we become like a conduit— a lightning rod. The energy has somewhere to go. The energy is no longer anger and fighting and destruction. Once we take responsibility, it ends.

I looked at how I carried around loss and sadness and came to a point where I realized that I carried this load every day. It was mine.

Grant and Rachel? They were fine. They were swimming in the sea of new love. I would be surprised if either of them thought of me much. This 'charge', this negative 'energy' was mine, and I was shouldering the load. I felt the weight of the injustice of it all, the unfairness of it all, and the sadness of it all.

It was my load, and for many months and even the early years, it was a heavy load.

Initially, there appeared to be no reprieve to my load; no answer to my misery and loss. Grant and I were not going to get back together. Full reconciliation with him was impossible. But I still had a heavy heart and loaded shoulders.

I came to understand that this was *my* load, and it was over to me to give myself relief.

It is ironic that the loss I suffered was so devastating for me, the outcome of that betrayal damaging to so many areas of my life; and yet there were so many times in the early stages when I was still willing to repair my relationship with him.

Such contradiction.

This is the 'heart' and 'head' thing again.

I think this was because Grant and I had so much history. Also, in the turmoil of the confusion and the highly emotional state, I just wanted all the pain to go away. Confronting the truth proved to be incredibly hard.

I had to steel myself and gave myself every chance of looking at the reality as much as possible; and yes, there were so many times that I needed to force myself to keep looking at what was real. For so long, I was in disbelief and would have loved to stick my head in the sand. But, sliding into the slope of pretense is just as hurtful in the long run.

Realistically though, in the early days and months, if Grant had come to me, explaining that leaving me was such a horrendous mistake and that he was so very sorry for the hurt he had inflicted, I think I could have been of a mind and seriously considered the possibility of staying with him. I'm being raw and honest here.

For me, this explains why my story has moments of back and forth in my viewpoints. The head and the heart have separate vantage points sometimes.

***

I was watching an interview on Oprah where she spoke of some of her childhood and areas where it could be considered that she needed and deserved more parental support and the question arose: did she forgive her mother? Her answer stuck with me. She replied that she now understood that her mother did the best she knew how to do.

Oprah says, *"Forgiveness is giving up the hope that the past could be any different. We can think that forgiving means accepting what has happened to us. It's more accepting that it has happened to us. Not accepting that it was okay for it to happen. It is accepting that it has happened."*

Oprah goes on to say, *'It's letting go, so that the past does not hold us prisoner. Forgiveness is like medicine that can heal our pain, bring us peace and ultimately to be free.*

*Forgiveness does not exonerate the perpetrator or justify their behavior. Forgiveness is the gift you give yourself".*

Sometimes, 'forgiveness' gets mixed in with 'letting go'. There is a difference. We can let go of hurt and betrayal but when it comes to forgiveness, real forgiveness, then this takes more from us.

It's time to take a harder look at the concept of forgiveness.

To readily say that you 'forgive' someone, is a positive way of looking at things, but it does not mean that the emotional charge of it has been handled. Actually, a rapid 'I forgive you' usually means that the person hasn't even begun to handle the emotional charge of it. It's more along the lines of 'Yes, I forgive you, (but brother, am I going to get you back)!'

We have to engage with the event at an emotional level, and that requires *feeling*.

Some may think that when we come to a place of forgiveness that now we are best buddies with our perpetrator. Not so.

Sometimes the resolution is to come to a place where we can say, 'I recognize for the love of self, that I don't want to be around you.' This can result in a great sense of freedom where we say, 'I don't have to be around you. Go live your life. I wish you well, but I don't want you in my sphere anymore.'

There is a sense of completion and freedom with that decision. That still is forgiveness. It is forgiveness and coming to a place of self-love that says, 'If you choose to continue with these destructive patterns, I don't want you in my space, but I wish you well on your journey.' Sometimes, it can simply be that their energy is not compatible with our own energy. That's okay. 'I don't have to change you. I don't have to fix you. I don't have to appease you, either. I can simply live my life away from you.'

Let them go.

Forgiveness can happen with just us involved. It does not need the other person to be present or even engage or agree.

The thing is, conflict requires two sides. If we have loosened our reins and come to a place where we made the decision that staying in this circus is damaging to us, then we are starting to disengage. The karma has ended with that person. They may go on to engage with someone else. We are only responsible for our own lines of energy and for the pattern that we engage in.

It is *our* load of sadness and resentment and betrayal and hurt that we need to deal with.

Forgiveness is recognizing that we need to stop carrying our load. Everyone—including the person or persons who inflicted the perceived injustice—carries their own loads. We are just responsible for our load. They can't help us. It's ours to hold on to, or ours to release.

An important aspect of this for me, was realizing that Grant did not need to be present for me to forgive, to end it. I did not need to say to him that I forgave him. I did this by myself and for myself. And as I say that, I don't know that I can fully forgive his actions that caused so much pain and disruption in my life; but somehow, once I saw that he was stuck in a pattern, that awareness allowed me to release myself from the chaos of it all. It was as though I was caught up in a whirlwind that I had become part of. But once I extricated myself—which allowed me to be separate from it and not be involved in the swirl and saw it for what it was—that started me on the path of experiencing some form of *acceptance*.

Ironically, within hours of my doing this, he phoned. He rang to chat. I was happy to hear from him. Not heart-beating happy that it was him on the phone; it was a neutral reaction, like hearing from a friend. There is no desire or romantic love within me for him anymore, but there remains an appreciation for the time we had together. Part of the 'forgiving' moment I had with myself was the clearly articulated decision that I did not need to experience him again in any form. In a karmic sense, I had reaped what I had sown but I had worked through the steps of taking responsibility for my own actions and harm that I had caused others in my past.

An important thing to recognize when it comes to forgiveness, is that the other person does not have to be present.
This is not necessarily something that is discussed between you and that other person. Forgiveness happens within you.
It's a decision made by you.

GAYNOR

# Chapter Forty-Three

# Can A Couple Be Okay With Each Other After Divorce?

Some of the following is quoted from the British TV series "the Split"

What is the secret to the good divorce?

They say that you never really know a person until you divorce them. But no-one tells you how hard divorce really is. And though we make vows to love and honor—For better or worse. In sickness and in health—Those vows are hard to keep.

Yet, while we put so much score on the wedding, the happy ending, the photos, the Instagram posts of the perfect honeymoon—we forget to put as much care and as much love into the way we divorce.

...And it certainly costs us more. More than any wedding.

(From my own experience, I felt that the cost was the loss of the way we treasured the memories, the photos...the loss of the shared stories that we laced our lives together with. The loss of the knowing and understanding silent looks).

It's easy to marry. Knowing how to divorce is hard.

There has to come a point where the divorce is finalized. For some, this is a moment of relief. A big full-stop marking the ending of what could be perceived as a huge mistake in their lives. For others, while the marriage is over, there might still be the entanglement, the complications, and the children that resulted from the relationship.

This is where your personal T—junction comes into play again. Yes, you can be 'right' for the rest of your life and hang on to how 'bad' your partner was and all of the energy charge and emotion that comes with that. Or, over time, you could lay down your weapons and realize that this person is going to be in your life for a long time due to the ties that bind: the children.

Some can do this. They place the mental welfare of their joint offspring above the shouting and the hurt and determine that they will remain civil and reasonably considerate.

There comes a time where our own mental and emotional welfare starts to take priority and we can let the upset stuff go, for our own future.

I know of a woman so bitter that her husband left her well over forty years ago, that she will be 'right' and he will be 'wrong' in her eyes until the grave. She lives on her own, but by God, she is 'right'! Imagine the color of the energy eating away at her insides.

We've seen that not all endings have the possibility of being civil, but a lot of endings can, over a little bit of time, be reasonable.

With each marriage or relationship, there was the time that those two people cared very deeply for each other and for whatever the network of reasons, it just didn't work out. But surely there has to be a time when we let it go? When we say 'hey, it just didn't work out' and live today as today, and not with the resentment, hurt and anger of the past.

# Chapter Forty-Four

# Meet Hubby #1

My first husband was Bryan. We married in 1980 and had the one daughter in 1982. Bryan was, and still is, a great man but after some years married, I knew it was right for me to end the marriage. I could no longer live with him. He was a really good person. But for me, the marriage was over.

Over subsequent years, I came to fully appreciate just how hurt he was that our marriage ended.

While we were no longer going to be husband and wife, he still wanted me to be in his life. He said that keeping me in his life was not just because we had a child, but because he cared for me. Actually, we cared deeply for each other. No longer in a deep romantic way, but we held a genuine caring. It was just the 'living together' thing that was no longer possible.

Bryan remarried and has been with his wife for many years now. We share grandchildren and family gatherings, and I am always warmed by their company. I am lucky, too, that his wife initially tolerated and came to fully understand what it is that Bryan and I have and does not feel threatened by it.

We stayed relatively close. We go to each other's social events, Christmases, even holidaying as larger families sometimes do. Actually, he and his wife came to Grant's and my wedding.

Bryan and I have always held a deep respect for one another, and it is that respect that sits at the very foundation of our relationship. Personally, I believe that if the core element of a relationship is respect, then that's a kind of glue that holds people together.

When Bryan and I parted, he came to crossroads of his own, his own 'T-junction'. He was hurt when our marriage ended and, at that time, told me that he determined that he had two choices. He could cut me out of his life altogether, or he could remain cordial and keep me in his life. He chose the latter. And thank goodness he did.

It is possible to remain friends when there is divorce, although this is not always the case with all relationship endings. In fact, I would estimate that most relationship endings are best with the big full-stop after them with no further contact.

For us, it was through Bryan's loving decision that we have maintained a wonderful bond to last a lifetime.

I looked at this when I was trying to recover from Grant leaving me and thought that maybe I could try and keep some form of relationship with Grant. While Grant and I were forced to attend the same events (family weddings and special occasions) in the early days, I did not like seeing him and Rachel together. It felt strange and unnatural to me. I was not neutral in my feelings. For a long time, there was a lot of hurt, and when he moved to Australia to live permanently with her, I felt a sense of relief that I was not going to bang into them at the same restaurant.

I found it so incredibly strange that initially, my feelings were so mixed up. Grant is a person who clearly has a pattern with women that he repeats and keeps repeating and so, logically, why would I want to join that circus?

That was my head talking.

But my heart took some time to stop aching. So, what was that about?

I think that it was because our marriage bank had a lot of credit in it. Together, we had dug the ditch of the not-so-good times, and at the time of the breakup, our future was cleared for lift off for much better times. And that was The Matakana Dream. For me, of course there was a huge loss. But I am okay now with the way my life is working out.

I am not at a point of being able to happily socialize with Grant and Rachel, so I guess not every story has an amazingly happy ending. But when he phones, which he does every few months, I feel okay to hear from him and happy to catch-up about the various family members.

When I look at my two marriages—both to very capable, strong men—I now feel very grateful that I have had two great loves in my life; two incredible experiences that I treasure, and I know that I am richer for having had them both.

One man I hurt deeply. The other man hurt me deeply. Neither relationship was better or worse. They were different. Both were incredible experiences for me and each has enriched me so very much.

## Chapter Forty-Five

# How Are Things Now?

The greatest realization for me through all of this is the classic 'living in the present'. We just have this one moment. And 'now' is actually all we have. We can't live in the future as that hasn't happened yet and we can't live in the past because that has gone. But we can take experiences from the past and take them forward as we carve and create our own future.

Our experiences are unique to us. Some are wonderful and some are not-so-good, and each event shapes who we are now. The real beauty is how we handled the dark times. How we trekked through sludge and molasses to find our way.

Most of us don't get through this lifetime without some form of sadness, disappointment, loss or grief. Our experiences are ours alone. What matters is how we deal with the lows and the knockdowns.

Sometimes, it's not possible to readily get up from a punch. That's okay, as long as we do get up again. Some of us can take a while to find our feet.

There's no deadline. We all move to different drum beats.

As I look back, I have come to comprehend that the change to my feeling better came from the decisions made each and every day. There is no magic wand that can make us instantly better, but there are ways to try to be able to feel better and ultimately genuinely be better, for ourselves.

Living alone and being content to do so can be rewarding, but only if we are okay with being alone. That comes from feeling comfortable with who we are, deep inside, at the core of ourselves. Our very essence. A space where we have confidence in our moral compass and our viewpoints. It's a wonderful place to be. For some, they are not built to be on their own…and that's okay, too. An ideal way to be in a relationship is when you know who you are and like who you are.

Contentment with self… It's the secret to real happiness.

"Someday, we'll forget the hurt, the reason we cried and who caused us pain. We will finally realize that the secret to being free is not revenge, but letting things unfold in their own way and own time. After all, what matters is not the first, but the last chapter of our life which shows how well we ran the race."

PAULO COELHO

# Epilogue

I have been asked to reveal when all of this occurred, how old I was when this happened and how long did my 'healing' take.

The eruption occurred in mid 2012. I was fifty eight at that time. Grant and I divorced in 2018. Ironically, I was the one who petitioned for a divorce. Grant was passive. I received an email from our solicitor with the final signed copy of our dissolution of marriage documents followed by the actual papers in the post. I never opened that envelope.

I can say that, for me, the physical pain of the initial shock lasted many months and I know I cried for about two years after my world blew apart... but I came through. Getting through is possible. Being happy again is very possible.

To put a time-frame around the healing process is not possible though. What is healing? When are we fully *healed*? We each move to our own timeline. Some are very happy again after a loss in a short space of time and others take a lot longer, so it would be unfair of me to number an amount of months or years that this process takes.

For me, my being on the trek from loss to contentment happened in steps and stages; moments and realizations, pockets of acceptance, shifts and changes most of which have been covered in this book.

I am now sixty eight and am the most content I have been in my life. I haven't remarried nor am I currently in any serious relationship but my head and heart are open should someone come rambling into my life again.

I am still in New Zealand. I live in my beautiful cottage amongst the native trees…

…and I'm happy.

www.ingramcontent.com/pod-product-compliance
Lightning Source LLC
Chambersburg PA
CBHW060647150426
42811CB00086B/2449/J